We are delighted to partner with
The Society for the Study of Social
Problems to publish the Agenda
for Social Justice.

Other publications available from
Bristol University Press and its imprint
Policy Press:

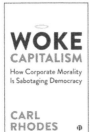  

Find out more at bristoluniversitypress.co.uk

Home of

P Policy Press

Our series and journals include:

Find out more at bristoluniversitypress.co.uk

AGENDA FOR SOCIAL JUSTICE 3

JUSTICE 3

Solutions for 2024

Edited by
Kristen M. Budd, Heather Dillaway,
David C. Lane, Glenn W. Muschert,
Manjusha Nair, and Jason A. Smith

First published in Great Britain in 2024 by

Policy Press, an imprint of
Bristol University Press
University of Bristol
1–9 Old Park Hill
Bristol
BS2 8BB
UK
t: +44 (0)117 374 6645
e: bup-info@bristol.ac.uk

Details of international sales and distribution partners are available at policy.bristoluniversitypress.co.uk

British Library Cataloguing in Publication Data
A catalogue record for this book is available from the British Library

ISBN 978-1-4473-7139-7 paperback
ISBN 978-1-4473-7140-3 ePub
ISBN 978-1-4473-7141-0 ePdf

FSC
www.fsc.org
MIX
Paper | Supporting
responsible forestry
FSC® C013604

Table of contents

President's welcome

Mary Bernstein

This volume exemplifies the mission of the Society for the Study of Social Problems to create rigorous empirical research that can be marshaled to solve the most pressing social problems facing society today. This volume focuses on a variety of institutions and issues including the criminal justice system and mass incarceration, health care, along with reproductive and transgender justice, education, immigration, housing and climate. The chapters examine how ideological and structural systems of racism, xenophobia, and transphobia shape these institutions, policies, and practices. By understanding the cultural and structural underpinnings of systems of inequality and domination, this research can be used to understand and ultimately reduce inequality, violence, and poverty. As social scientists, we can provide the building blocks for understanding complex systems of power and domination. Thus, this book exemplifies the best that emancipatory social science has to offer, not only identifying and understanding social problems but using empirical research to advance progressive social change.

Editorial introduction

Kristen M. Budd, PhD

The Society for the Study of Social Problems (SSSP) and its members work toward alleviating the most pressing social problems in the United States and globally—enduring work to improve our human and social conditions. Through research, teaching, activism, and public education, we pursue various avenues of public sociology to remedy society's social ills. As part of the SSSP's mission to create a more just world, this project—the *Agenda for Social Justice*—was born from Professor Robert Perruci's 2000 Presidential Address.

As the 48th President of the SSSP, Dr Perrucci challenged us to infuse our sociological work into the public sphere. He called upon all of us to advance an agenda for social justice using the sociological perspective grounded in rigorous research methodology and theory. The knowledge created by the SSSP members should be and must reach beyond our professional organization and academic institutions. Within the SSSP, the Justice 21 Committee, composed of a team of SSSP members, self-published the first *Agenda for Social Justice* volume in 2004. Since 2016, the volumes have been published by Policy Press, our academic publisher based at the University of Bristol (UK), whose values closely align with those of the Justice 21 Committee and the SSSP.

The *Agenda for Social Justice: Solutions for 2024* continues to embody Dr Perrucci's call to disseminate actionable and science-based solutions using the sociological tools at our disposal. This volume coincides with the United States's presidential election and includes 16 topical chapters on social problems facing the US today. Readers will learn about social issues related to the criminal legal system, education, precarious social conditions (such as food and housing insecurities), and health/healthcare. An additional "think piece" asks readers to attune themselves to these social challenges unfolding in a constant state of culture wars. Given the expansiveness of social problems in the US, this volume is far from complete. Indeed, there is more work to be done.

A wide array of experts contributed to this edited volume, including those from higher education—graduate students, post-doctoral fellows, and faculty at all ranks—as well as researchers and advocates working in academic centers, think tanks, and non-profit organizations. Their work and expertise help us understand these pressing social problems—their definition and scope, the evidence documenting the extent of each social problem, and, notably, the actionable solutions for reducing, mitigating, solving, or abolishing them.

The SSSP's Justice 21 Committee, who work together to bring these volumes to fruition, invites readers to learn more about what we can do to create social change to improve our communities and, more globally, the social conditions for all humankind.[1]

Note

[1] Perrucci, R. (2001) Inventing social justice: SSSP and the twenty-first century. *Social Problems*, 48(2): 159–67.

About the Society for the Study of Social Problems

The Society for the Study of Social Problems (the SSSP), is an academic and action-oriented professional association, whose purpose is to promote and protect social science research and teaching about significant social problems in society. Members of the SSSP include students, faculty members at educational institutions, researchers, practitioners, and advocates.

Some of the SSSP's core activities include encouraging rigorous research, nurturing young sociologists, focusing on solutions to the problems of society, fostering cooperative relations between the academic and the policy and/or social action spheres.

If you would like to learn more about joining the SSSP, reading our publications, or attending our annual conference, please visit the SSSP website: www.sssp1.org.

Finally, please consider supporting the SSSP, a non-profit 501(c)3 organization which accepts tax deductible contributions both in support of its general operations and for specific purposes. It is possible to donate to the SSSP in general, but it is also possible to donate in support of specific efforts. If you would like to encourage the kind of public sociology represented in this book, please consider supporting the efforts of the Justice 21 Committee. For information on contributing, please visit www.sssp1.org/index.cfm/m/584/.

Notes on contributors

Charity Anderson is Academic Director of the Clemente Veterans' Initiative Newark, a humanities course focused on themes of war and reconciliation for military-connected civilians. Her research interests include urban education, poverty and inequality, and transformative education for disenfranchised adults and youth. She holds a PhD in social work from the University of Chicago.

McKenzie Berezin is a sixth-year counseling psychology doctoral fellow at New York University. Her research seeks to reduce the multi-level impact of systemic inequity on youth through collaborative systems change efforts. Specifically, her research supports local and national initiatives to disrupt youth pathways across child serving systems in partnership with court- and community-based organizations through the implementation of gender- and trauma-responsive practices and policies. Her work also supports the efforts of local and international programming that investigates the structural drivers of health disparities among adolescents and how they can be bolstered through community-based programming and policy change.

Drew Bonner's research engagements focus on the policies and practices of community health, education, and food access. He supports uplifting equitable initiatives for underserved communities through his research on racial equity in food access, collaboration with organizations, and evaluation collaboratives focused on community-based food access and nutrition education. In addition to this work, Drew Bonner is a sociology PhD student at George Mason University (GMU) and a graduate researcher within the Center for Social Science Research at GMU. His academic engagements interrogate how food insecurity and health disparities become reproduced and institutionalized, being motivated and inspired through his engagement with social justice, food justice, and research seeking to promote community wellness.

Sarah Jane Brubaker is a sociologist and Professor of Criminal Justice and Public Policy at the L. Douglas Wilder School of Government and Public Affairs at Virginia Commonwealth University. She studies and teaches about gender violence and juvenile justice from feminist, social justice, and intersectional lenses. She has received federal grants to reduce violence against women on college campuses and to provide programming and support to girls involved in the juvenile justice system, working with community activists, and publishing her work in scholarly venues.

Kristen M. Budd, PhD, is Research Analyst at The Sentencing Project. She is the lead researcher on their voting rights campaign and contributes research to their campaign to end extreme sentences. She has spent the majority of her career researching crimes of a sexual nature, including law and policy responses, public opinion, as well as patterns and predictors related to incidents of sexual assault. Her work at The Sentencing Project has been featured on *Yahoo News* and other regional news media outlets. Dr Budd earned an undergraduate degree from Indiana University South Bend and a master's and doctorate in sociology from Purdue University.

Kristen Lagasse Burke, MA, is a PhD candidate in sociology at the University of Texas at Austin. Her research focuses on inequality in childbearing patterns, addressing access to contraception and abortion as well as trends in the birth rate in the United States. In Texas, her research has involved collaborations with community organizations that provide reproductive health services and has resulted in op-eds, policy briefs, and academic publications. Before graduate school, Kristen worked as a research assistant at the Guttmacher Institute and served as an AmeriCorps VISTA in Spartanburg, South Carolina where she helped open a free health clinic.

Hayley Carlisle is a Criminology, Law and Society doctoral student at George Mason University and a graduate research assistant at the Early Justice Strategies (EJS) Lab. She received her Master of Science from American University in Justice, Law & Criminology, specializing in justice and public policy. Before starting her doctoral journey at George Mason University, Hayley worked for the DC Department of Corrections. During that time, she designed and supported programs for returning citizens and incarcerated residents in the DC Jail.

Brooke Cordes is a rising senior at Villanova University with majors in political science and criminology and a minor in business. She has participated in a variety of social justice groups, including the Philadelphia Justice Project. Following graduation, she intends to continue her passion for justice reform in law school.

Heather Dillaway is Dean of the College of Arts and Sciences and Professor of Sociology at Illinois State University, US. Previously, she completed a BA in sociology and history at Cornell University, an MA in sociology at the University of Delaware, and a PhD in sociology at Michigan State University. Her research focuses on women's menopause experiences and reproductive health experiences of women with physical disabilities. She participates in many editorial projects, including coediting an issue of *Gender & Society* on intersectionality and disability (in 2019), a book titled *Musings on Perimenopause and Menopause: Identity, Experience, and Transition*

(Demeter Press, 2021), and volume 14 of *Research in Social Science and Disability* (Emerald, 2023).

Nazgol Ghandnoosh, PhD, is Co-Director of Research at The Sentencing Project. She conducts and synthesizes research on criminal justice policies, with a focus on racial disparities, lengthy sentences, and the scope of reform efforts. She regularly presents to academic, practitioner, and general audiences and her work has also appeared in *The Washington Post*, *The New York Times*, and WNYC's On the Media. Dr Ghandnoosh earned an undergraduate degree from the University of Pennsylvania and a doctorate in sociology from the University of California, Los Angeles.

Gabriela Gonzalez is Assistant Professor in the department of Justice Studies at San José State University. Her research examines the nature and impact of punishment, law, and inequality in the United States. Specifically, Gabriela's work analyzes experiences of confinement, both physical forms such as incarceration, solitary confinement, and immigration detention, and non-physical forms including checkpoints and legal barriers that block access to services, in order to understand the consequences of punishment for not only the individual, but the entire family.

Ashley N. Gwathney is a Doctor of Social Work and a licensed School Social Worker in New Jersey. She has worked with Cornwall Center of Metropolitan Studies, Rutgers Mountainview Communities, and the NJ-STEP (Scholarship and Transformative Education in Prisons) programs. Her research interests include restorative justice, urban education, and punitive school discipline.

Lance Hannon is Professor in the Department of Sociology and Criminology at Villanova University. He has published dozens of articles in scholarly journals about the intersection of race, crime, and justice. These include works in the *American Journal of Sociology*, *Social Forces*, *Social Problems*, *Criminology*, and *Justice Quarterly*.

Monique H. Harrison is currently a postdoctoral research fellow at the University of Pennsylvania and an education research scientist at Harvard University, where she leads a research/practice partnership with Harvard's Math Department. She is a sociologist of education who focuses on choice and decision-making. Her work examines how different factors, including gender, race, and socio-economic status, influence academic predilections, course choices, and undergraduate pathways. She received her PhD in Sociology of Education from Stanford University in 2022. Her dissertation focused on first year choices and stratification.

Sydney Ingel is a Criminology, Law, and Society doctoral student at George Mason University and a graduate research assistant at the Early Justice Strategies (EJS) Lab and the Center for Correctional Excellence (ACE!). She previously attended Quinnipiac University for her BS in criminal justice and psychology and then attended George Mason University for her MA in Criminology, Law, and Society.

Dana M. Johnson, MPAff, PhD, is Senior Associate Research Scientist at Ibis Reproductive Health. Her research focuses on changing public policy to make abortion care more accessible, affordable, and acceptable. Her research has been cited in amicus briefs to the US Supreme Court, and her writing on abortion and contraception has been published by *The New York Times*, *Teen Vogue*, and other outlets. Prior to graduate school, she was a grassroots organizer for a reproductive rights organization in the upper Midwest. She now lives in Texas and serves on the Board of Jane's Due Process, an organization that ensures legal representation for pregnant and parenting minors in Texas.

Tiffany D. Joseph is Associate Professor of Sociology and International Affairs at Northeastern University. Her research explores: race, ethnicity, and migration in the Americas; immigrants' health and healthcare access; the impacts of public policy on individuals; and the experiences of faculty of color in academia. She is author of *Race on the Move: Brazilian Migrants and the Global Reconstruction of Race* (Stanford University Press, 2015), and her work has been published in various peer reviewed journals and national media outlets.

Katie Kerstetter's research focuses on the intersections of food, education, social policy, and maternal and child health. She is particularly interested in amplifying marginalized voices and identifying and addressing structural barriers to more equitable food, education, and healthcare access. She takes a collaborative and participatory approach to research. She enjoys partnering with organizations working to distribute resources more equitably and involve those most directly affected by inequities in programming and policy decisions. She has expertise and experience in qualitative and mixed methods research, needs assessments, and program evaluations. Katie holds a PhD in sociology from George Mason University and a master's in public policy from the University of Maryland College Park. She is the author of *How Schools Meet Students' Needs: Inequality, School Reform, and Caring Labor* (Rutgers University Press, 2022).

Jeanne Kimpel, PhD, is Assistant Professor of Sociology at Molloy University. She is also Director of the Dr Joan Reidy Merlo Community

Research Institute where her recent work has included evaluating a grant to serve the needs of at-risk youth in a local Long Island community. Dr Kimpel has been teaching courses on racial disparities and inequality for 17 years with the intent of providing students with critical thinking and research skills needed to examine racial, ethnic, and gender inequalities. Her scholarly work has included research in the area of residential segregation, housing, social networks, and violence towards nurses in acute care psychiatric facilities.

David C. Lane is Associate Professor in the Department of Criminal Justice Sciences at Illinois State University. He holds a PhD in sociology from the University of Delaware. He is the author of *The Other End of the Needle: Continuity and Change among Tattoo Workers*. He has previously published research on art theft, tattooing and tattoo work, and natural hazards, along with numerous legal reports and exhibits about issues in tattoo work. His current research focuses on social control in disaster response phases and the relationship between tattooing and bodily autonomy.

Glenn W. Muschert is Professor of Sociology in the Department of Public Health and Epidemiology at Khalifa University (جامعة خليفة), Abu Dhabi, United Arab Emirates. He previously served on the faculty at Miami University and Purdue University (US), and as a visiting scholar at Erzincan University and Atatürk University (Turkey). His research focuses on the metaverse, digital inequalities, sustainable development, and the resolution of social problems. He has published numerous scholarly volumes, peer-reviewed articles, and chapters in academic volumes in sociology, media studies, social justice studies, and sustainable development. He serves as Secretary of the Society for the Study of Social Problems (SSSP).

Manjusha Nair is Associate Professor of Sociology at George Mason University, US. Before this, Dr Nair taught at the National University of Singapore. Dr Nair completed a PhD in sociology from Rutgers University and a master of philosophy in economics from Jawaharlal Nehru University in India. Dr Nair's research and teaching interests are in globalization, political sociology, comparative and historical sociology, development, labor movements, India, China, Ethiopia, and South Africa. Dr Nair's publications include an award-winning book, *Undervalued Dissent: Informal Workers' Politics in India* (SUNY Press, 2016), and articles in *Development and Change, Critical Sociology*, and *International Labor and Working-Class History*.

Lindsay Redditt is a rising senior at Villanova University with majors in political science and criminology and a minor in Spanish. She is active in the Student Government Association, Black Student Union, Black Law Student Association, and Academic Reform Committee.

Ashley C. Rondini is Associate Professor of Sociology at Franklin & Marshall College, where she is an affiliate faculty member in public health, Africana studies, and women's, gender, and sexuality studies. She is a former ASA Spivack post-doctoral congressional fellow, and past recipient of the ASA's Fund for the Advancement of the Discipline Grant, and Carla B. Howery Teaching Enhancement Grant. Her work has been published in *Social Problems*, *JAMA Pediatrics*, *The American Journal of Bioethics*, *Sociological Forum*, *Social Science and Medicine*, *The DuBois Review: Social Science Research on Race*, *Humanity & Society*, *Teaching Sociology*, *Sociology Compass*, and *Contexts*.

Raquel E. Rose is a doctoral candidate in Counseling Psychology at New York University. Her research seeks to understand the impact of systemic trauma, resource precarity, and deficit-based narratives around ethnic minority youth on psychosocial outcomes particularly in the mental health, education, and legal fields. Raquel focuses on the effective implementation, evaluation, and scalability of interventions and participatory programs with youth who are legal system-impacted to inform multi-disciplinary efforts to change systems/policy and promote equitable youth-centered service delivery and innovation.

Tony R. Samara is Senior Policy Organizer at the Right to the City Alliance and previously worked with the movement for tenants' rights in the San Francisco Bay Area. He holds a PhD in sociology from the University of California, Santa Barbara and was an associate professor of sociology at George Mason University between 2011 and 2014.

Blake R. Silver is Associate Professor of Sociology and Director of Educational Pathways and Faculty Development at George Mason University. He is the author of *The Cost of Inclusion: How Student Conformity Leads to Inequality on College Campuses* (2020), which won an American Educational Studies Association Critics' Choice Book Award and the NASPA Faculty Council Outstanding Publication Award. His second book, *Degrees of Risk: Navigating Insecurity and Inequality in Public Higher Education* is forthcoming with the University of Chicago Press.

Jason A. Smith is Research Affiliate at the Center for Social Science Research at George Mason University, US. Dr Smith's research focuses on race and media exclusion, with overarching themes including issues related to access and representation for communities of color in various institutional and organizational spaces. Previous research has been published in *Ethnic & Racial Studies*, *Sociology of Race & Ethnicity*, and *Studies in Media and Communication*.

Teresa A. Sullivan is University Professor of Sociology at the University of Virginia. She previously taught at the University of Michigan, the University of Texas-Austin, and the University of Chicago. She is a demographer who does research on labor force demography and on the US census. The author or co-author of seven books and more than one hundred articles and chapters, she teaches undergraduate courses in demography, social problems, and the politics of data. She earned her PhD from the University of Chicago and her bachelor's degree from James Madison College at Michigan State University.

Meredith Van Natta is Assistant Professor of Sociology at the University of California, Merced. Her research explores immigration and social welfare policies in the United States, as well as the intersection of citizenship and science, medicine, and technology policy. She is the author of *Medical Legal Violence: Health Care and Immigration Enforcement Against Latinx Noncitizens* (NYU Press, 2023), and her work has been published in a variety of interdisciplinary peer reviewed journals.

Sophie Webb is a PhD candidate at the University of California, San Diego. Her research examines the pathway from ethics to implementation in public health, and she is interested in understanding how decisions made in allocating and prioritizing limited health resources can impact health inequities.

Elroi J. Windsor, PhD, is Professor of Sociology at the University of West Georgia. Windsor's research and teaching interests focus on gender, sexuality, and the body. In 2023, Windsor co-edited *Male Femininities* (NYU Press, 2023), and previously co-edited multiple editions of *Sex Matters: The Sexuality and Society Reader* (W. W. Norton). Since 2023, Windsor has served as the Executive Officer for the Society for the Study of Social Problems. They earned an undergraduate degree from Chatham College and a master's and doctorate in sociology at Georgia State University.

Acknowledgments

We, the editors, have the privilege to work with an exceptional group of people. Our team effort to cultivate this volume includes our authors, whom we thank for sharing their expertise. We offer our gratitude to Michele Koontz and Elroi Windsor, the SSSP administrative and executive offices, respectively, and the SSSP Editorial and Publications Committee. They assist us in executing crucial components throughout the year as well as support the work of the Justice 21 Committee in general. We value their expertise and continuous support. We give additional thanks to Policy Press, our long-standing publishing partner. We collaborate to disseminate publicly accessible research to alleviate social problems and promote social change. Finally, to our SSSP members: We look forward to our continued collaboration with you to improve this world.

PART I

Crime, law, and policy

ONE

From blame to criminalization: Black motherhood and intimate partner violence

Sarah Jane Brubaker

The problem

Black women are marginalized by systemic oppression in the United States across multiple social institutions. Historically, Black mothers have been viewed as unfit based on various negative stereotypes that have shaped their interactions with systems in the US. The "welfare mother/welfare queen," "jezebel," "matriarch," and "crack mother" are examples of derogatory images of Black women prevalent throughout US popular culture. Such images have worked to objectify and dehumanize Black women, blame them for particular social problems facing their communities, and work against viewing them as victims or deserving of empathy and compassion.

Black women are more likely than White women to experience intimate partner violence (IPV), and ironically, legislation initially and ostensibly intended to protect victims of violence has come to be used against them. Black mothers who are victims of IPV are particularly harmed by the criminalization of IPV and fetal endangerment. *Mandatory arrest* and *failure to protect* laws are disproportionately used to arrest Black women who are victims of IPV and engage in self-defense. Feticide and *fetal personhood laws*, originally enacted to protect pregnant women from partner abuse, have been used to justify drug testing vulnerable and marginalized pregnant women and charging them with fetal homicide after miscarriage. These laws rely on and reinforce negative stereotypes and controlling images to arrest, convict, and incarcerate increasing numbers of Black mothers who are marginalized, victimized, and oppressed by social systems.

In this chapter, I provide evidence of the overcriminalization of Black mothers who experience IPV by identifying specific social conditions and laws that contribute to this problem. I then explore three types of solutions and provide specific examples of each.

Research evidence

In this section, I lay out evidence of the problem of criminalization of Black mothers who are victimized by IPV. I provide brief summaries of overcriminalization and the IPV and pregnancy experiences of Black women. I then identify specific forms of legislation that have facilitated the process of criminalization through their framing of and response to IPV and fetal endangerment.

Overcriminalization

- In recent years, there has been a growing recognition of the problem of excessive criminalization in the United States. This process began with the founding of the "United States of America," when White European property-owning men seized land from Native Americans and established a criminal legal system to protect their property and interests by exploiting and oppressing members of powerless and marginalized groups through a wide range of legalized practices such as chattel slavery. Since that time, cultural ideologies have justified policies and procedures that prioritize punishment, assume a clear distinction between offenders and victims, and dehumanize and objectify marginalized groups. From the system of slavery to the Jim Crow era to mass incarceration, criminalization has taken a variety of forms but has continued to dominate our legal system. Since the 1980s, politicians and policy makers have promoted a "Tough on Crime" stance justifying the war on drugs and accompanying "three strikes" laws and mandatory arrest statutes contributing to mass incarceration.

Intimate partner violence and pregnancy

- Black women are more likely than White women to experience IPV intimate partner violence and less likely to seek services or support from the criminal legal system or victim service agencies due to a lack of trust, fear of mistreatment, and structural and economic barriers.
- Black women are less likely than White women to have access to prenatal health care and more likely to experience pregnancy complications, including low birth weight babies, miscarriages, and stillbirths.

Legislation

- Mandatory arrest and "failure to protect" laws have been implemented to criminalize IPV. The goal of mandatory arrest laws is to ensure that individuals are held accountable for perpetrating domestic violence, even when victims are afraid to report. Failure to protect laws aim to ensure that children are not harmed by living in environments where they witness or experience family violence. While the intention of each statute is worthy, they have been selectively enforced and differentially applied and often are used against victims.

- Black women are more likely than White women to be arrested for self-defense against their abuser and for failure to protect their children from living in an abusive home.
- The recent overturning of *Roe v. Wade* through the Dobbs Decision has exacerbated fetal personhood laws initially intended to protect pregnant women from domestic violence. Such laws have been used to surveil, arrest, and convict pregnant women for potentially harming their fetuses through drug use or when they miscarry.
- Black women are more likely than White women to be forced to undergo mandatory drug testing during pregnancy, even when there is no history of drug abuse. They are also more likely to be charged with fetal homicide when they experience a miscarriage.

Recommendations and solutions

Scholars and activists have called for decriminalization in multiple areas. Solutions can be framed through three broad approaches that I apply to the problem of criminalization of Black mothers who experience IPV.

System reform

Many solutions to overcriminalization call for system reform and focus on changes to existing laws and practices of law enforcement, adjudication, and punishment. These strategies do not challenge our current system ideologically or philosophically but continue prioritizing punishment while attempting to lessen its impact. Here are specific examples as applied to Black mothers:

- We need to change existing laws and the enforcement practices that harm Black mothers. Some states, for example, have begun to require that victims' histories of abuse be taken into account when they are arrested for violence in the home through mandatory arrest since they often act in self-defense against long-term abuse. One example is New York State's Domestic Violence Survivors Justice Act (DVSJA), passed in 2019, which allows for shorter sentences when offenses are related to victimization.
- Fetal endangerment laws should also be changed so that a miscarriage is not viewed as an attempt to terminate a pregnancy or as a result of harm or neglect since there is no scientific way of determining the cause. The Notice of Proposed Rulemaking (NPRM) that the Office of Civil Rights

issued in April of 2023 would help by strengthening the Health Insurance Portability and Accountability Act (HIPAA) Privacy Rule protections to prevent the disclosure of private health information that would be used to "identify, investigate, prosecute, or sue patients, providers, and others involved in the provision of legal reproductive health care, including abortion" (hhs.gov).

- Child welfare and health care systems should operate independently of the criminal legal system rather than being required to implement failure to protect and fetal endangerment laws. Service providers should not be required to report and share data with law enforcement officers and prosecutors regarding the support and care provided to women. These systems should focus exclusively on providing services to those they are designed to support and not be expected or required to become additional arms of the criminal legal system.

- When enforcing fetal personhood laws, limits should be placed on police discretion regarding drug testing of pregnant women so that only those with a history of drug abuse and demonstrating clear evidence of risk to the fetus are tested. Police should be trained to recognize and resist bias against Black women.

- When enforcing both mandatory arrest and fetal personhood laws, limits should be placed on prosecutorial discretion to bring charges against women in abusive relationships or who are pregnant without clear evidence of violations. Prosecutors should also be prepared to counter bias and be subject to increased scrutiny and performance reviews. The progressive prosecution movement has begun to identify specific policies to support IPV victims that focus on diversion programs, refusing to cooperate with other carceral systems and restorative justice.

Restorative justice and harm reduction

Others are calling for changes in how we conceptualize punishment more broadly, shifting from retributive and punitive approaches to those based on restoration and accountability, such as restorative justice frameworks that have been implemented successfully in various settings. These approaches focus on entire communities rather than individuals and reject current ideological and philosophical views of punishment and changes in practice.

- Restorative approaches redefine justice to focus on accountability rather than punishment. These frameworks require strong community foundations where people care about each other. The practices focus on the harm done to others, including the harm done to the entire community and what those harmed need to heal. Practices engage both those who cause harm and those who are harmed in the response and healing process and emphasize mutual respect, dignity, and empathy. The Center for Court Innovation (2019) assessed restorative justice approaches to IPV in four case studies across Hawaii, Minnesota, and Maine and found positive outcomes for survivors, abusers, and communities. Focusing on harm reduction rather than punishment broadens our response to providing addiction treatment and services to pregnant women rather than arresting them for using drugs. Another form of harm reduction is providing mental health services to women coping with various stressors during pregnancy and in their lives generally so that they can care for themselves and others.

Transformative justice and enhanced community accountability

Still, others argue that our systems are fundamentally flawed and founded on systemic racism and oppression and must be abolished. Such approaches are grounded in transformative justice and abolitionist frameworks that call for defunding the police and carceral systems and shifting resources from the criminal legal system to broader social supports and investment in communities, including affordable housing, quality public education, and access to health care. This approach further argues for a shift from system-based punishment to community accountability.

- Reallocating funds from punishment to support would provide all women with access to quality reproductive and prenatal care to control their fertility and ensure safe and healthy outcomes for all. This is in sharp contrast to our current context that denies many women decision-making autonomy, access to safe and affordable contraception, including abortion, and access to quality prenatal care, then punishes women for pregnancy outcomes that are consequences of systemic deprivation, neglect, and abuse.
- A community approach also includes ensuring that all members are cared for and their basic needs are met, including safe housing, a living wage, and child care. Such an inclusive approach humanizes all community members in ways that invoke compassion and care, making it more difficult to impose and justify harsh punishment.
- Community accountability is a social movement that seeks to restore and strengthen communities, drawing on the histories and knowledge of indigenous women and women of color, to resist formal systems' responses to violence. Two key organizations leading this work are Incite! Women of Color Against Violence and Creative Interventions. They lead conferences and workshops and have published a toolkit with practical strategies to stop IPV without relying on formal systems.

Conclusion

Black mothers who experience IPV bear the brunt of criminalization in the US and are disproportionately harmed by laws, policies, and procedures intended to protect victims. They are arrested and convicted for defending themselves, for being trapped in abusive environments with their children, and for experiencing adverse pregnancy and childbirth outcomes. A broad array of strategies and solutions must be undertaken to address this problem and seek social justice, from system reforms to harm reduction to social activism and community accountability. The solutions exist; we must demand the political will to realize them.

Key resources

Center for Court Innovation (2019) *A National Portrait of Restorative Approaches to Intimate Partner Violence: Pathways to Safety, Accountability, Healing, and Well-Being*. Available from: https://www.innovatingjustice.org/sites/default/files/media/document/2019/Report_IPV_12032019.pdf

Dirks, S. (2022) Criminalization of pregnancy has already been happening to the poor and women of color. *NPR*. Available from: https://www.npr.org/2022/08/03/1114181472/criminalization-of-pregnancy-has-already-been-happening-to-the-poor-and-women-of

Finoh, M. and Sankofa, J. (2019) The legal system has failed black girls, women, and non-binary survivors of violence: Black women, girls, and non-binary people are seldom seen as victims. *ACLU*. Available from: https://www.aclu.org/news/racial-justice/legal-system-has-failed-black-girls-women-and-non

Harp, K. L. H. and Bunting, A. M. (2020) The racialized nature of child welfare policies and the social control of black bodies. *Social Politics*, 27(2): 258–81.

If/When/How (2016) *Women of Color and the Struggle for Reproductive Justice*. Available from: https://vawnet.org/sites/default/files/materials/files/2016-08/Women-of-Color-and-the-Struggle-for-RJ-Issue-Brief.pdf

Maye, E. (2021) Black women bear the brunt of criminalized pregnancy and motherhood: here's why we can't afford to ignore it. *The Root*. Available from: https://colorofchange.org/press_release/the-root-op-ed-black-women-bear-the-brunt-of-criminalized-pregnancy-and-motherhood-heres-why-we-cant-afford-to-ignore-it/

Meyerson, C. (2018) For women of color the child welfare system functions like the criminal justice system. *The Nation*. Available from: https://www.thenation.com/article/archive/for-women-of-color-the-child-welfare-system-functions-like-the-criminal-justice-system/

Rabin, R. C. (2023) Black pregnant women are tested more frequently for drug use, study suggests. *New York Times*, [online] April 14. Available from: https://www.nytimes.com/2023/04/14/health/black-mothers-pregnancy-drug-testing.html

U.S. Department of Health and Human Services (2024) Regulatory initiatives: HIPAA Privacy Rule and reproductive health care. Available from: https://www.hhs.gov/hipaa/for-professionals/regulatory-initiati ves/index.html#:~:text=On%20April%2012%2C%202023%2C%20 OCR,or%20sue%20patients%2C%20providers%20and

TWO

Curbing pretextual traffic stops to reduce racial profiling

Lance Hannon, Lindsay Redditt, and Brooke Cordes

The problem

A pretext is a lie, a false justification to avoid accountability. A pretextual stop occurs when a police officer pulls someone over for a minor traffic violation merely as an excuse to investigate whether the person has any outstanding warrants or contraband. Promoted as an integral part of the war on drugs in the 1990s, the practice continues to be widespread throughout the United States. Since nearly everybody commits some form of technical violation when they drive, police officers have the de facto ability to investigate people at random. However, these fishing expeditions are not conducted randomly. Instead, police officers try to maximize their chances of finding someone with contraband or an outstanding warrant by targeting people believed to be more involved in serious crime. Ultimately, by asking police officers to follow their "gut" rather than evidence-based procedure the practice of pretextual stops enables racial profiling.

Study after study has shown that people of color are much more likely to endure fruitless investigations during traffic stops.[1,2,3] This is especially true for stops justified by non-moving violations, such as having items hanging from the rearview mirror. While frequently touted as a way to take guns off the streets, traffic stops for minor offenses almost never deliver illegal firearms. Moreover, while the proceeds from pretextual stops are extremely meager, the costs are absolutely enormous.

Consider, for example, the high-profile case of Tyre Nichols in Memphis, a young Black man who lost his life to police violence when he was pulled over for an alleged traffic violation about a mile from his home. In that tragic case, a specialized police unit with a crime-fighting mission appropriated the routine of a generic traffic cop—avoiding the legal requirement that they first establish reasonable suspicion of criminal behavior. That specialized unit, known as the Scorpion Team, was deactivated after nationwide protests. Nevertheless, the practice of pretextual policing continues to be pervasive.

The research evidence is clear that traffic stops for minor infractions: (1) rarely lead to any evidence of criminal wrongdoing, (2) exhibit worse racial disparities than stops for dangerous driving behaviors, (3) increase mutual mistrust between police and citizens, and (4) are a net harm rather than benefit to officer and public safety. We present some of this evidence in the next section.

Research evidence

Analyzing data for over 60 million highway patrol stops (covering 20 states), researchers from the Stanford Open Policing Project reported that, on average, only about 5 percent of stops led to an arrest, with the most common initial stop justification being speeding.[4] Search rates were about twice as high for Black and Hispanic drivers, relative to White drivers. Using a sophisticated statistical test, the researchers also found that, for most jurisdictions, the evidentiary threshold to search Black and Hispanic drivers was lower than what was needed for searching Whites. Overall, the researchers concluded that people of color experienced more stops and more unsubstantiated searches.

A study examining over 300,000 vehicle stops in Philadelphia found even starker results.[5] In particular, the researchers noted that (1) only about 2 percent of stops led to an arrest, (2) in a city that was 40 percent Black, more than 70 percent of stops involved Black drivers, (3) unproductive searches of Black drivers were several times more common than all searches of White drivers, and (4) Black drivers were significantly more likely to be pulled over when external conditions made it easier to discern the driver's race. A likely reason why stops and searches in Philadelphia were more inefficient and unequal relative to the national average is that, rather than speeding, the vast majority of stops in the city were legitimated based on non-moving/equipment violations.

The enforcement of equipment violations appears to be especially racially disparate, as indicated in a recent report from the San Francisco Bay Area Planning and Urban Research Association.[6] While 12 percent of traffic stops for White drivers involved equipment issues such as a broken taillight, 31 percent of traffic stops for Black drivers were justified this way. While the number one reason for stops of White drivers was failure to halt at a stop sign, the number one reason for Black drivers was an incorrectly displayed license plate. The report also noted that only a small percentage of Black drivers actually received a ticket for the violation legitimating the stop—suggesting an alternative purpose for the encounter.

A comprehensive research study in the Kansas City metropolitan area concluded that racial disparities in stop and search rates were almost entirely concentrated in investigatory stops—discretionary detentions based on minor motor vehicle code violations that end up being inquiries about serious crime.[7] In contrast, traffic-safety stops, such as those for excessive speed, did not exhibit meaningful differences across racial and ethnic groups. The researchers noted that, when surveyed, people of color were deeply resentful of investigatory stops involving minor infractions. However, for all groups, traffic safety stops for dangerous behaviors did not appear to erode trust in the police.

An analysis of millions of traffic stops in Connecticut, Illinois, Maryland, and North Carolina corroborated the core conclusion of the Kansas City research: to reduce racial disparities, police departments should prioritize traffic safety "must stop" violations and de-prioritize "could stop" investigatory detentions.[8] Police Chief Harold Medlock of Fayetteville, North Carolina asked his officers to do just that. More specifically, his reform initiative rewarded officers when they focused their traffic stop efforts on serious moving violations, such as blowing through stop signs or running red lights. A rigorous evaluation of this intervention revealed significant reductions in both racial disparities and traffic fatalities, while leaving the crime rate unchanged.[9] Another sophisticated evaluation concluded that Medlock's initiative reduced assaults against officers because it decreased the prevalence of confrontational stops for minor transgressions.[10]

In addition to initiatives by individual police chiefs, some states and cities have attempted to legislate reform. Analyzing temporal variation in the legality of pretextual stops in the state of Washington, a recent study demonstrated that racial disparities in traffic stops were lowest when state law was most restrictive of the practice.[11] The study's authors concluded that decoupling traffic-code enforcement from crime-fighting agendas would sharply reduce racial inequality.

Recommendations and solutions

A key reason for the ubiquity of pretextual stops is that the practice's constitutionality was affirmed in *Whren v. United States* (1996). In that decision, the U.S. Supreme Court ruled that such stops do not violate the Fourth Amendment (which protects against unreasonable searches). More generally, the Court suggested that claims about an officer's hidden intentions cannot be the basis for a constitutional challenge. Still, the Court's ruling left open the possibility of state and city-level reforms of the practice. In the wake of *Whren*, policy efforts restricting pretextual stops have taken two general forms: (1) enforcement directives by local criminal justice officials and (2) state and municipal legislative actions. Next we will discuss some promising existing efforts, and we make recommendations for future localized plans.

- Elect/hire police chiefs and DAs that recognize how pretextual stops undermine safety.

As was seen in Fayetteville, NC, having the right police chief can make a big difference (see note 9). Although often characterized as one of the first successful "bans" on pretextual stops, it is more accurate to describe Chief Medlock's initiative as a *reprioritization*. That is, the emphasis was on what officers should be doing with their limited time, not what officers are prohibited from doing. The core message was that stopping people involved in dangerous driving behaviors is more effective at promoting public safety than stopping and investigating people arbitrarily. Furthermore, every fruitless pretextual stop is time taken away from preventing serious accidents and responding to serious crime.

In larger jurisdictions, police chiefs will likely have their executive power curtailed by a variety of stakeholders. Nevertheless, having a police chief that is at least non-oppositional to reform efforts spearheaded by other community organizations is crucial. For example, in contrast to the cooperation demonstrated by police chiefs in Philadelphia, Los Angeles, Minneapolis, Seattle, and Oakland, the police chief in Pittsburgh simply refused to train his officers to comply with an ordinance limiting stops for minor offenses. Criminologists have long lamented the challenge of implementing effective criminal justice reform. A key lesson is that the police are a closed community; they will subvert reform efforts advocated [exclusively] by outsiders (see note 3).

Like the police, prosecutors are a tightknit group possessing a considerable amount of discretionary power—power that can be used to stymie or spur reform. Several recently elected district attorneys have used their positions to help curtail the tactic of pretextual stops. For example, John Choi, the district attorney for Ramsey County in Minnesota declared that "to focus on the greatest threats to public safety, and enhance procedural justice, we will decline to prosecute charges arising from non-public-safety stops or searches of vehicles based solely on consent."[12] In this decree, non-public safety violations included transgressions like expired license plate stickers, loud mufflers, objects hanging from the rearview mirror, cracked windshields, prohibited window tint, and a single missing headlight or taillight. Similar declarations were made by progressive prosecutors in San Francisco and in Chittenden County, Vermont and Ingham County, Michigan. The intended purpose of such statements is to encourage the police to not waste time on pretextual policing.

In our view, these public stances are positive because they draw attention to this important issue, and they *might* make police officers think twice. Still, our strongest recommendation in terms of personnel is to elect mayors who will hire police leadership truly open to evidence-based reform. As mentioned earlier, the evidence is quite clear that pretextual stops are counterproductive, especially considering other public safety options. Police chiefs are in a unique position to motivate their officers to choose a more effective approach, not simply eschew an ineffective one.Most importantly, police chiefs should direct officers with traffic duties to focus on serious moving violations that are a clear threat to public safety (such as significant speeding, blowing through a red light or stop sign, traveling the wrong way down a one-way street, and so on). Second, officers who mostly conduct traffic stops should be assigned to neighborhoods based on traffic data, not crime data. When traffic-safety officers are deployed to neighborhoods based on a high level of crime, the officers quite reasonably assume that their primary mission there is to investigate criminal behavior. Third, police chiefs should dismantle reward structures that emphasize arrests and citations for career advancement. Instead, executive command staff should specify that other duties, especially those related to police–community relations, will be tangibly appreciated. Finally, police executives should hold officers and their immediate supervisors accountable for data indicating continued use of pretextual stop tactics (for example, a very high rate of unsuccessful searches or frisks and very low rate of ticketing).

- Promote legislative limits on police discretion in traffic stops.

A weakness of reform efforts driven by the visions of individual administrators is that they are often unsustainable. Reform-minded leaders will come and go. The institutionalization of reform through legislation enables stability. Perhaps the most obvious solution is to legalize all discretionary minor offenses, leaving just serious violations under the purview of law. However, as seen in the decades-long efforts to legalize marijuana, legalization is a far more challenging endeavor than decriminalization (both in the terms of procedural constraints in the law and political polarization). Thus far, existing attempts at legislating constraints on police discretion in traffic stops have taken a more practical decriminalization approach—one that leaves minor offenses on the books but changes how violations are enforced.

For example, rather than attempting the daunting task of overhauling the motor vehicle code, the 2022 Driving Equality and Accountability Ordinance (DEAO) in Philadelphia cleverly works within an established Pennsylvania legal framework. The DEAO does not legalize minor infractions commonly used in pretextual stops, such as having a broken taillight, recently expired inspection/registration, or item hanging from the rearview mirror. Instead, the DEAO exploits the currently existing legal distinction between primary and secondary violations—originally employed to stop police officers from pulling people over solely for not wearing a seatbelt—to shorten the list of violations officers can use to justify traffic stops. As with failing to wear a seat belt, the remaining (secondary) violations are still illegal, but they cannot be used to initiate the detention and investigation of a motorist. In our view, the DEAO is exemplary in its ease of implementation and ability to withstand legal challenge.[13]

Comparable city ordinances are in effect or planned in Berkeley, Memphis, Oakland, and Brooklyn Center, MN. Employing nomenclature like Philadelphia's, the Memphis law is known as the Driving Equality Act. For Brooklyn Center, the ordinance is referred to as the Daunte Wright and Kobe Dimock-Heisler Community Safety and Violence Prevention Act. We recommend that future initiatives consider combining the themes in these titles. More specifically, we propose an integrated narrative that draws attention to the fact that equity and safety are not mutually exclusive—they are mutually reinforcing. One possibility is something like: the Driving Equality and Community Safety Act.

Besides cities, several states have introduced laws aimed at reducing pretextual stops by recategorizing certain infractions as secondary (not stop worthy). As of this writing, these include Connecticut, Virginia, Oregon, and Washington.[14] Similarly, some states have enacted laws protecting motorists against unreasonable searches of vehicles. For example, unlike many states, consent searches in New Jersey are not valid unless there is reasonable and articulable suspicion that the driver has engaged in, or is planning, criminal activity. The logic behind requiring reasonable suspicion in addition to a motorist's consent is that, in the moment, many people may not understand their right to refuse an officer's request to search. Like New Jersey, we recommend that states legislatively limit situations where officers can request consent searches without first establishing reasonable suspicion or probable cause. Additionally, states should mandate that consent be written—thus giving the citizen time to reflect on their decision to give up one of their fundamental rights (see note 3). At a minimum, officers should be obliged to inform motorists of their right to refuse search requests (as is done in Colorado). Local community organizations and broader social movements should push for these legislative reforms by engaging in direct conversation with elected representatives at town halls, amassing signatures on petitions, harnessing the power of social media, and peacefully protesting. After such legislation is passed, it is important for activists to stay informed about how the policies are being implemented on the ground.

- Require data collection and schedule regular data monitoring with diverse stakeholders.

Importantly, besides delineating a focused list of primary versus secondary violations, the DEAO law in Philadelphia also wisely mandates that the police department publicize detailed data for all stops (not just those leading to criminal investigations). This component of the legislation makes several significant contributions. First and foremost, it allows for an independent assessment of whether the initiative is working, as well as the monitoring of potential side or substitution effects (for example, an increase in pedestrian stops or a new type of pretextual vehicle stop). Second, the data component promotes transparency and associated legitimacy. Third, rather than overburdening the police with new record keeping duties, the DEAO reasonably requires the release of information already collected for other purposes.

This information includes the date, time, and location of the stop (longitude and latitude); year, make and model of the vehicle; the drivers' race, ethnicity, and gender, and the race, gender, and ethnicity of passengers; the primary vehicle violation; any and all secondary violations; whether a warning or citation was issued; whether occupants of the vehicle were frisked or searched; whether occupants of the vehicle were arrested; whether the vehicle stop resulted in the recovery of contraband, and the specific nature of any recovered contraband (such as firearm versus narcotics). In addition to these data fields, we strongly recommend that future ordinances require the release of anonymized officer ID numbers linked to each stop. While this requirement will likely meet stiff resistance from police unions, it is important for community members to be able to see the range of variability at the officer level (bad apples and good apples in comparative perspective with average apples).

Ordinances should also require police departments to develop audit procedures to ensure that the public database is kept reasonably accurate and complete. To promote accessibility, we recommend that raw data files be downloadable in a comma-delimited format. Additionally, public data dashboards/visualizations should be designed to facilitate basic analysis of patterns and trends in key variables. It is important that data interfaces be user-friendly to encourage independent investigations by members of the public and press. See the Stanford Open Policing Project for an exemplary data archive and web interface (note 4).

Beyond regular collaboration with citizen police oversight committees, we further recommend that police departments proactively reach out to local journalists, community organizations, and academics to assist them in understanding the nuances of the data. Transparency is more wholly achieved when important information is communicated before it is requested—or uncovered.

Conclusion

In addition to voting for the right leaders and laws to curb the vehicular equivalent of stop and frisk, citizens may need to take to the streets to effect change. There is a long history of peaceful protests initiating impactful criminal justice reform in the United States. As mentioned earlier, it was mass protest that led to the quick dismantling of the Scorpion crime-fighting traffic unit in Memphis. Still, we believe that systemic change in the (mal) practice of pretextual policing will require a multifaceted, incremental, and evidence-based approach. Indeed, Memphis is an exemplar in this regard, with city councilmembers unanimously passing the Driving Equality Act after negotiation and compromise with police administrators. This law, based on an ordinance in Philadelphia, appropriately narrows the list of infractions that police officers can use to justify pulling someone over. The goal of such legislative efforts matches that of earlier initiatives by progressive police chiefs—reduce racial inequality by making traffic stops truly about traffic safety.

Notes

[1] Fagan, J. (2022) No runs, few hits, and many errors: street stops, bias, and proactive policing. *SSRN Electronic Journal*. https://doi.org/10.2139/ssrn.4052926

[2] Gross, N. (2020) Opinion. It is possible to reform the police. *The New York Times*, [online] September 8. Available from: https://www.nytimes.com/2020/09/08/opinion/police-reform-biden.html

[3] Harris et al (2023).

[4] Pierson et al (2020).

[5] Hannon, L., Neal, M., and Gustafson, A. R. (2021) Out-of-place and in-place policing: An examination of traffic stops in racially segregated Philadelphia. *Crime & Delinquency*, 67(6–7): 868–90.

[6] Spur (2023) Putting an end to biased traffic stops in San Francisco. Available from: https://www.spur.org/events/2023-08-10/putting-end-biased-traffic-stops-san-francisco

[7] Epp et al (2014).

[8] Roach, K., Baumgartner, F. R., Christiani, L., Epp, D. A., and Shoub, K. (2022). At the intersection: race, gender, and discretion in police traffic stop outcomes. *The Journal of Race, Ethnicity, and Politics*, 7(2): 239–61.

[9] Fliss, M. D., Baumgartner, F., Delamater, P., Marshall, S., Poole, C., and Robinson, W. (2020) Re-prioritizing traffic stops to reduce motor vehicle crash outcomes and racial disparities. *Injury Epidemiology*, 7(1): 3.

[10] Boehme, H. M. (2023). The influence of traffic stop policy changes on assaults against officers: a quasi-experimental approach. *Policing: A Journal of Policy and Practice*, 17: paad002.

[11] Rushin, S. and Edwards, G. S. (2019) An empirical assessment of pretextual stops and racial profiling. *SSRN Electronic Journal*. https://doi.org/10.2139/ssrn.3506876

[12] Ramsey County (2021) Charging policy regarding non-public-safety traffic stops. Available from: https://www.ramseycounty.us/sites/default/files/County%20Attorney/Charging%20Policy%20Regarding%20Non-Public-Safety%20Traffic%20Stops%209.8.21.pdf

[13] City of Philadelphia (2021) Implementation of driving equality policy. Available from: https://www.phila.gov/media/20211109145453/executive-order-2021-06.pdf

[14] The Policing Project (n.d.).

Key resources

Epp, C. R., Maynard-Moody, S., and Haider-Markel, D. P. (2014) *Pulled Over: How Police Stops Define Race and Citizenship*. The University of Chicago Press.

Harris, D. (2002) *Profiles in Injustice: Why Racial Profiling Cannot Work*. The New Press.

Harris, K., Hecker, S., Iguina González, C., and Jain, A. (2023) The road to driving equality: a blueprint for cities to reduce traffic stops. *SSRN Electronic Journal*. https://doi.org/10.2139/ssrn.4517462

Pierson, E., Simoiu, C., Overgoor, J., Corbett-Davies, S., Jenson, D., Shoemaker, A. et al (2020) A large-scale analysis of racial disparities in police stops across the United States. *Nature Human Behaviour*, 4(7): 736–45.

The Policing Project (n.d.) Pretextual traffic stops. Available from: https://www.policingproject.org/pretextual-traffic

The Vera Institute of Justice (2021) *Investing in Evidence-Based Alternatives to Policing: Non-Police Responses to Traffic Safety*. Available from: https://www.vera.org/downloads/publications/alternatives-to-policing-traffic-enforcement-fact-sheet.pdf

Weisburd, D. (2017) Proactive policing and crime control. *Nature Human Behaviour*, 1(10): 707–8.

THREE

Pay to talk: the financial barriers, consequences, and solutions to prison and jail communication

Sydney Ingel and Hayley Carlisle

The problem

Barriers to external communication for incarcerated loved ones affect more than 549,100 individuals incarcerated in jail and over 1.2 million incarcerated in prison yearly in the United States. Loved ones, particularly family members, are often forced to pay exorbitant prices for various communication services lest they lose contact with those behind bars. A 2018 report published by FWD.us estimated that 1 in 2 adults has had an immediate family member incarcerated for at least one night. Approximately 1 in 4 US adults have had a sibling incarcerated, 1 in 5 adults experienced parental incarceration, 1 in 7 adults have had an incarcerated spouse or co-parent, and 1 in 8 adults had their child incarcerated.

The financial costs of maintaining contact with incarcerated individuals far outstrip what one would pay to communicate with a non-incarcerated person. For example, according to the Prison Policy Initiative's annual prison and jail phone rate surveys, a 15-minute in-state prison phone call in 2021 cost an average of $0.15 to $2.10, depending on the state. Depending on the locality, an in-state phone call from jail costs an average of $0.93 to $5.47 per 15-minute call.

Video visitation is a new option for communication, allowing visits to occur from external locations. In some jurisdictions, video visits can take place anywhere with a computer and webcam if scheduled in advance with an approved visitor. The costs can be far higher than phone call rates, with a 30-minute video call costing $9.95 in some jurisdictions. Though there are significant benefits—convenience, improved access to loved ones, and reduced recidivism[1]—visitors often report that video calls are impersonal, low-quality, and subject to technology problems that may cut visits short.

Emails and other electronic messages from carceral facilities permit communication with less scheduling than phone or video calls but still cost money for incarcerated individuals. The Federal Bureau of Prisons operates TRULINCS, or the Trust Fund Limited Inmate Computer System, which incarcerated persons use to send messages for $0.05 per minute spent on the messaging platform. Other privately-operated services, such as J-Pay, offer similar services by purchasing an electronic "stamp" to send their message.

Unsurprisingly, low-income families are disproportionately affected by the cost of communication services with their incarcerated loved ones. Not only do they have fewer resources to maintain communication, but low-income families are over-represented in the criminal-legal system. A 2018 report by Looney and Turner at the Brookings Institute found that for persons incarcerated between 2009 and 2013, the average income 2 years before incarceration was $12,780, with only 44 percent of incarcerated individuals reporting any earnings. Compared to families with an income over $100,000 per year, families making under $25,000 per year are 61 percent more likely to experience having an immediate family member incarcerated.

Research evidence

This section will discuss the financial impact of available communication methods for incarcerated individuals and the negative consequences (for example, loss of contact, suicidality, institutional misconduct, recidivism) that result when incarcerated individuals and their loved ones cannot afford to pay to talk. With the high costs of phone calls, e-messages, and video visits, incarcerated persons must decide between several undesirable options:

Fund calls themselves

- Opportunities to generate income behind bars are minimal, and the wages tend to be low. Incarcerated persons can expect between $0.13 and $0.52 per hour for traditional prison jobs. Industry jobs, which represent only 6.5 percent of prison inmate jobs, pay slightly higher, between $0.30 and $1.30 per hour.[2]
- Little to no information is available for jail inmate wages due to the variation in local facilities and the unpredictable length of stays.

Rely on family and friends

- Research on correctional telecommunication service providers suggests that kickbacks shared with facilities through negotiated contracts amplify costs for loved ones and those incarcerated.
- Collect calls typically pose a higher cost-per-minute than prepaid calls. However, prepaid options often require access to the Internet or credit

cards, both of which may not be accessible for economically disadvantaged loved ones.
- Adding money to inmate accounts for prepaid call rates poses significant fees for those who must wire money. To add $50 to an inmate account, Western Union charges an additional $12 transaction fee.[3]

Go without

- The psychological impact of lack of contact with family is well established. Studies cite depression, strain on relationships, difficulty maintaining contact with children based on relationships with their custodian or guardian, and general loss of contact over time.[4] Incarcerated persons who experienced a near-lethal suicide attempt reported lower social support than individuals with no suicide attempt history.[5]
- When contact is cut off from loved ones, institutional misconduct increases as incarcerated persons without a support network experience anger and violence.[6] Individuals may seek alternate sources of support, increasing the likelihood of association with drug trafficking networks.[7]
- Loss of contact between incarcerated persons and their spouses is associated with divorce due to the separation and strain on relationships.[8]
- While incarcerated, phone calls protect against recidivism; research finds that recidivism is reduced by frequent family contact.[9] Without contact with loved ones, the millions of people released from jails and prisons each year may be at increased risk of recidivating.

Recommendations and solutions

With millions locked behind bars each year in the United States, incarceration affects a significant portion of the population directly or indirectly. The exorbitant costs to communicate with people incarcerated in prisons and jails have financial, social, and recidivist effects. To alleviate these adverse effects on incarcerated individuals and their families/friends, we present several recommendations and solutions for reducing the costs of phone calls, video visitation, and e-messages.

Provide no-cost or at-cost phone calls

- This problem can be solved via legislation making prison and jail phone calls free, as recently seen in Connecticut and California state prisons. In 2021, Connecticut became the first state to pass legislation requiring prison phone calls to be free and prohibiting state agencies from collecting any revenue from communication agencies. California followed suit, and in 2022, Governor Newsom ratified a law making phone calls from California prisons free of charge. In doing so, Connecticut and California have shifted phone call costs from incarcerated people and their families to the state-run Department of Corrections. These states show that legislative efforts to curb prison communication costs can succeed. However, this may be a stretch for some states, and it does not address county-run jails, so at a minimum, prisons and jails should make the cost of their phone calls comparable to what someone not incarcerated would pay for a phone call.

- During the COVID-19 pandemic, most jails and prisons restricted in-person visitation. To facilitate communication with loved ones despite the restrictions, many facilities implemented free methods of communication. According to a study in 2021 by Dallaire and colleagues, 48 out of 50 state corrections departments instituted free phone calls, offering between 1 and 10 free calls averaging 11 minutes each. Out of the 25 states with pre-existing video chat programs, 16 provided an average of one 19-minute call per week. Physical mail received subsidies in 10 states, offering between 1 and 12 free postage stamps per week, while 15 states provided free electronic mail with an average of 2.6 weekly emails. Offering free or low-cost communication services is not impossible, as these COVID-19 modifications prove. Rather than returning to overpriced communication services, facilities must continue this trend.

Legislate uniformity in phone call costs

- In January 2023, President Biden signed the *Martha Wright-Reed Just and Reasonable Communications Act* into law, confirming the authority of the Federal Communications Commission (FCC) to cap interstate and intrastate phone calls. Currently, the FCC caps interstate phone calls as follows: $0.12 per minute in prisons and $0.14 per minute in large jails. However, the FCC has until 2024 to decide the caps for intrastate phone call prices. These caps should not exceed the prices already set for interstate phone calls (no more than $0.14 per minute) and should be set as low as possible. Ideally, intrastate phone call prices would be capped at $0.10 per minute for both prisons and large jails. After these new caps are set for intrastate phone calls, the next legislative step is to expand the reach of the *Martha Wright-Reed Just and Reasonable Communications Act* to include small- and medium-sized jails. Such standardization would provide complete uniformity among carceral institutions and ensure that no matter where someone is incarcerated in the US, they receive equitable and reasonable phone call prices.

Stop using expensive, carceral-designed video visitation software

- Many prisons and jails use video visitation services provided by companies like J-Pay, who specifically design their services for use in prisons and jails. However, these carceral-designed software programs are often more expensive and of lower quality than video conferencing software widely and freely available to the public. For example, Zoom's Basic plan is free and allows unlimited video meetings, up to 40 minutes each. Like J-Pay, all Zoom requires is that both parties have access to computers with webcams and the Internet. Unlike J-Pay, Zoom does not need the person on the receiving end of the video call to go through the complicated process of creating an account, often a barrier that loved ones face. To use Zoom, video recipients do not have to have an account; they have to do nothing except click on the link provided to them by the sender. Rather than partnering with companies who charge incarcerated individuals for their service, prisons, and jails can use the free programs already out there that have proven quality. Prisons and jails can set up free accounts and allow 40-minute video visitation sessions for incarcerated individuals. Zoom has security features to secure meetings (such as password-protected links), and correctional staff can easily record and monitor meetings. This concept is not new, and due to the COVID-19 pandemic, jails in New York and Texas, along with Pennsylvania and Kansas prisons, have successfully used Zoom for both video visitation and educational programming.

Stop using expensive, carceral-designed e-messaging services

- Although many companies provide free e-messaging services, whether that be email (Gmail, Outlook, Yahoo) or text messages (GoogleVoice, WhatsApp), many prisons and jails use costly e-messaging services designed and provided by companies that specifically market their services to prisons and jails (such as TRULINCS and J-Pay). The fees associated with carceral-designed e-messaging services can be costly because they are unregulated, and the companies have no restrictions on what they can charge. It is inequitable to force incarcerated individuals to pay for services that would otherwise be free for those not incarcerated. Prisons and jails do not have to partner with these predatory companies to maintain security and surveillance of e-communications. Prisons and jails can partner with companies like Gmail or Outlook to create accounts that they have administrative control and surveillance over. Businesses also use multitudes of outside monitoring and surveillance software to monitor their employees, which could be adapted to surveil the e-messages that incarcerated individuals send and receive. While these outside companies still charge fees for these types of services, the service fees prison and jail agencies would have to pay are minimal compared to what incarcerated individuals currently pay.
- Alternate communication services designed for carceral spaces without the traditional cost exist. Nonprofit startup Ameelio offers free calling and

the first established user-friendly web messaging services for incarcerated persons. With digital literacy as a paramount barrier to formerly incarcerated individuals upon release, new internet users can maintain contact with loved ones while developing skills to improve their transition into the increasingly digital community.

Amplify the voices of incarcerated persons and their loved ones

- Advocacy groups like Worth Rises and the Color of Change include exorbitant phone call costs in their platforms, often led by loved ones affected by the high cost of consistent communication. Other organizations track the ongoing problem across the United States, including the Prison Phone Justice Project. Stories written by incarcerated and formerly incarcerated individuals published by The Marshall Project, a non-profit news agency focused on justice, highlight the firsthand experience of choosing between necessities and calling home. Sharing the stories and calls for action by those affected by excessive communication costs ensures that the lived experience is heard and recognized.

Conclusion

With close to 2 million people incarcerated in prisons and jails each year in the United States, pay-to-talk issues affect the lives of millions of parents, children, and significant others who struggle to maintain contact with incarcerated loved ones. The financial burden of maintaining communication between incarcerated individuals and their non-incarcerated loved ones far outstrips the cost of communication between two non-incarcerated individuals. To alleviate this financial burden and boost the benefits that come from increased communication (such as maintenance of relationships, reduction in mental health symptoms, reduced institutional misconduct and recidivism), we suggested several ways that prisons/jails, businesses, advocacy groups, and governments can address the pay-to-talk crisis going on in carceral settings.

Notes

[1] Duwe and McNeeley (2021).
[2] Turner et al (2022).
[3] Arguelles and Ortiz-Luis (2021).
[4] Travis, J. and Waul, M. (2003) *Prisoners Once Removed: The Impact of Incarceration and Reentry on Children, Families, and Communities.* The Urban Institute.
[5] Pratt, D. and Foster, E. (2020) Feeling hopeful: can hope and social support protect prisoners from suicide ideation? *The Journal of Forensic Psychiatry & Psychology,* 31(2): 311–30.
[6] Celinska, K. and Sung, H.-E. (2014) Gender differences in the determinants of prison rule violations. *The Prison Journal,* 94(2): 220–41.

[7] See note 6.
[8] See note 4.
[9] Barrick, K., Lattimore, P. K., and Visher, C. A. (2014) Reentering women: the impact of social ties on long-term recidivism. *The Prison Journal*, 94(3): 279–304.

Key resources

Arguelles, P. and Ortiz-Luis, I. (2021) Bars behind bars: digital technology in the prison system. SSRN. http://dx.doi.org/10.2139/ssrn.3812046

Charles, P., Poehlmann, J., Kerr, M., Jensen, S., and Pritzl, K. (2023) Supported remote video visits for children with incarcerated parents in the United States. *Current Issues in Criminal Justice*, 4: 473–93.

Dallaire, D. H., Shlafer, R. J., Goshin, L. S., Hollihan, A., Poehlmann-Tynan, J., Eddy, J. M., and Adalist-Estrin, A. (2021) COVID-19 and prison policies related to communication with family members. *Psychology, Public Policy, and Law*, 27(2): 231–41.

Duwe, G. and McNeeley, S. (2021) Just as good as the real thing? The effects of prison video visitation on recidivism. *Crime & Delinquency*, 67(4): 475–97.

Kukorowski, D., Wagner, P., and Sakala, L. (2013) Please deposit all of your money: kickbacks, rates, and hidden fees in the jail phone industry. Prison Policy Initiative. Available from: https://www.ojp.gov/ncjrs/virtual-libr ary/abstracts/please-deposit-all-your-money-kickbacks-rates-and-hid den-fees-jail

Murdoch, D. J. and King, L. L. (2020) 'Not feeling like a caged animal': prisoner perceptions of a remote video visitation system. *Journal of Crime and Justice*, 43(2): 212–27.

Shlafer, R. J., Davis, L., Hindt, L., Weymouth, L., Cuthrell, H., Burnson, C., and Poehlmann-Tynan, J. (2020) Fathers in jail and their minor children: paternal characteristics and associations with father-child contact. *Journal of Child and Family Studies*, 29: 791–801.

Turner, J., Rosenblat, M. O., Guruli, N., Flores, C., Desch, S., El Tayeb, K. et al (2022) *Captive Labor: Exploitation of Incarcerated Workers*. Available from: https://chicagounbound.uchicago.edu/cgi/viewcontent.cgi?arti cle=1003&context=ghrc

Wessler, M. (2023) *SMH: E-Messaging in Prison*. Prison Policy Initiative. Available from: https://www.prisonpolicy.org/reports/emessaging.html

Wildeman, C., Comfort, M., Enns, P., Goldman, A., Fitzpatrick, M., Lee, H. et al (2018) *Every Second: The Impact of the Incarceration Crisis on America's Families*. Available from: https://everysecond.fwd.us/downloads/everysec ond.fwd.us.pdf

Immigration enforcement: the impact of crimmigration on mixed-immigration-status families in the US and the need for reform

Gabriela Gonzalez

The problem

Forced familial separation via detention and deportation is a looming threat facing the 6 million US-citizen children who currently live in households with at least one undocumented parent. Today's immigration landscape is characterized by a complex proliferation and intensification of existing immigration enforcement tactics at the federal, state, and local level separating tens of thousands of children from their parents and producing irreparable harm. In FY 2022 alone, Immigration and Customs Enforcement (ICE)— carried out 142,750 arrests, imprisoned a daily average of 30,000 individuals in one of the nation's immigration prisons, and deported over 70,000 persons. While these numbers are lower than record highs of 2019 (nearly a quarter million removals), rates have steadily increased each month since early 2022 as the world recovers from a global pandemic. Likely, we will continue to see increases in the imprisonment and removal of non-citizens in the forthcoming years.

Many of these detentions and deportations are made possible via "crimmigration." Although criminal law and immigration law are two separate systems, crimmigration is a term used by scholars to describe the process of blending the two whereby non-citizens who are convicted of a criminal offense may also have their current and future immigration statuses jeopardized. Specifically, the Illegal Immigration Reform and Immigrant Responsibility Act of 1996 (IIRAIRA) created a loophole for immigrants to experience dual punishment for the same act by placing all non-citizens who are arrested by police (criminal law) at risk of imprisonment in a detention facility and removal proceedings (civil law). Second, IIRAIRA intensified immigration consequences by categorizing numerous criminal law violations as "aggravated felonies". Contrary to what the name suggests, an aggravated felony does not indicate the action is violent in nature or causes greater harm to an individual or society. Rather, it merely signifies that the person who committed the act is a non-citizen. As a result, that person may be removed from the US. Third, this law applies retroactively. Today, many immigration arrests are executed for law violations dating back to the early 1990s. Alarmingly, a criminal conviction is not necessary for the ramifications of IIRAIRA to apply. Anyone who has been merely charged with a criminal law violation, even if the charges are dropped or the person is found not guilty in a court of law, is vulnerable to deportation. As a result, millions of families have been permanently severed due to crimmigration practices.

Every immigrant in the US is a member of a family unit; many are parents to US citizens. Given the interconnectedness of undocumented persons to their US-born children, the increasingly punitive nature of immigration policy in the US continues to yield negative and long-lasting impacts for thousands of mixed-immigration-status families[1] (hereafter mixed-status).

Research evidence

Consequences for children of detained or deported immigrants

Detention, deportation, and crimmigration practices more broadly, yield significant consequences for the entire household, especially for children. A growing body of scholarship including work by Gulbas et al,[2] Vargas et al,[3] and Golash-Boza[4] documents the ways in which US-citizen children in mixed-status families experience material, psychological, and educational hardships when a parent is forcibly removed from the home by the state. Immediately upon arrest, the family experiences a simultaneous loss of income (often from the primary breadwinner) and burden of added expenses related to imprisonment (such as legal representation and court-related costs, commissary, phone communication, and visitation). This financial hardship may lead to housing and food insecurity, especially if the non-detained parent is also undocumented and therefore may be fearful to seek out state or private agency support.

The arrest of a parent by immigration authorities may produce physical and psychological aftereffects. A growing number of studies including such by Patler and Gonzalez,[5] Chaudry,[6] and Dreby[7] have found that children may suffer from trauma, particularly if present at the time of a parent's immigration arrest, or if the arrest was a violent encounter. In addition, ambiguity, shame, and stigma are associated with forced parent-child separation. According to one study by Rojas-Flores and colleagues,[8] children whose parent is currently in immigration detention or has been deported are more likely to develop symptoms of anxiety, depression, and attention deficit/hyperactivity problems. This population is also more likely to report symptoms of PTSD. Finally, research by Gonzalez and Patler[9] suggests children with detained or deported parents are vulnerable to loss of a supportive school network due to their reluctance to share their family's situation with school-based adults, which may lead to academic failure or disruption in their academic trajectories.

Consequences for all children of undocumented immigrants

The consequences of crimmigration are long-reaching and endured by all children with an undocumented parent even if a parent is not physically imprisoned in a detention facility or removed from the country. US citizen children with undocumented parents experience economic instability due to a parent's blocked opportunities for employment. Recent work by Cruz-Nichols et al[10] also suggests that this population is less likely to access critical services including healthcare for fear of exposing an undocumented family member. Lastly, among children with likely undocumented parents, research by Amuedo-Dorantes and Lopez[11] suggests that the intensification of immigration enforcement raises children's probability of repeating a grade as well as their likelihood of dropping out of school altogether.

This growing body of scholarship on immigrants and their families therefore highlights the ways in which the intensification of immigration enforcement is experienced not only by non-citizens in ICE custody, but by a much larger population. Immediate legislative action must be taken to impede further harm.

Recommendations and solutions

Under the current system of immigration control, millions of US citizens in mixed-status families will continue to experience negative consequences of law enforcement. This section outlines the role of different state and non-state actors in shielding youths from the social and material harms of parental immigration imprisonment.

Measures to help youth thrive

- Community organizing

    Community-based organizations (CBOs) play a meaningful role (as non-state actors) in minimizing the harms of parental detention and deportation. They must continue to promote the overall well-being of children with undocumented parents. A first step is to raise awareness about immigrants' rights during encounters with ICE. CBOs should continue to host Know Your Rights workshops to distribute accurate information about the powers and limits of ICE agents. This includes informing the public of their right to not open the door unless an immigration agent presents a signed judicial warrant, distinguishing between said judicial warrant (signed by a US federal judge) v. an immigration warrant (signed by an immigration agent)—which does not hold the same authority—identifying ruses that immigration officers use to impersonate police in order to gain access to one's home, and identifying safe spaces from which ICE cannot arrest someone (such as churches and schools).

Hotlines that receive tips and verify checkpoints or heavy law enforcement presence have become popular amidst the rise of immigration enforcement. This allows residents to practice vigilance and avoid encounters with any law enforcement agency, therefore minimizing the possibility of arrest and subsequent transfer to ICE authorities. In addition to CBO's posting about ICE sightings online, teaching the public how to safely record an interaction as a bystander may prevent someone from being taken into custody, and at minimum, help identify the person who was apprehended and locate their family.

CBOs must also create opportunities to engage young people in obtaining correct information about the law. Social media can be a great tool. Via online platforms, information about workshops, trainings, local, state, and federal resources and more about immigrant rights can be delivered in age-digestible formats (such as videos, reels, infographics, pictures). Considering the diversity of the US population, information must also be shared in multiple languages across platforms.

As likely agents of political socialization, CBOs should create and expand youth organizing programs to involve young people in campaigns that address issues important to them including educational inequalities, environmental justice, juvenile justice, immigrant rights, and more. Learning how to speak to congressional representatives, participating in safe demonstrations, and creating platforms to have their voices heard will equip youth with the information and tools to fight for equity and social justice, and help them protect their families and loved ones from oppressive regimes.CBOs play a key role in deportation defense. This includes raising awareness about a particular case through social media, organizing phone zaps—an influx of calls to any authority telling them to do something about an issue (for example, to not deport an individual from their community), influencing local politicians to formally express support for a constituent facing deportation (either by accompanying the person to an appointment with an ICE officer in order to discourage that person's apprehension, or writing a letter of support to the judge on their behalf), and so forth. These efforts have shown to be fruitful and must continue.Lastly, CBOs can mitigate the suffering imposed via parental detention by assuring immigrants that it is safe to seek emergency assistance and benefits for them and/or their US-born children. In addition, providing assistance including economic (petty cash), food, housing, and much needed psychological support for the non–detained spouse and children in the immediate aftermath of an arrest is critical to protecting their well-being. If the organization does not offer these services, they can support the family in the referral process to an agency that does, particularly those that provide a service at low or no cost to the client. In this way, the psychological impact to children immediately following a parent's apprehension can be alleviated.

• School-based support

The wellbeing of children with undocumented parents at risk of deportation is also the responsibility of schools. Educators should receive comprehensive training on the demographic they serve and be informed about the potential of familial separation via immigration enforcement. Immediately upon noticing changes in a student's behavior or academic performance, teachers should connect with the student's caregiver to understand the causes of said changes and identify support mechanisms. School-based adult support can be a key protective factor for child well-being during parental detention and deportation.

Subject tutoring should be made available to students during and after school so that their grades are not jeopardized during parental detention/deportation. Students involved in extracurricular activities must be given the support to remain engaged, and opportunities must be created to involve those not already active in art, sports, or music as these activities have been found to promote academic success. CBOs can support by offering programming for young people, as well as parent classes including English proficiency and promote school, district, and state advocacy around issues affecting their children's schooling.

Outside of the classroom, psychological counseling must be offered to protect the student's cognitive development. Youth living through a parent's detention or deportation may feel confused, sad, distrustful, and need healthy avenues to vent and cope with their emotions. If the scope of need is beyond the capacity of school-based support, staff must work collaboratively with the child's caregiver and, with assistance of CBOs, facilitate referral to accessible psychological services in the community at low or no cost to the family.

Educators must also recognize that support is needed long-term as the length of time a parent will be detained is unknown, and the threat of deportation both precedes an arrest and looms well beyond release from an immigration prison. To that end, communication must be maintained among and between academic institutions as students matriculate from one grade to the next and from one school to another (elementary to middle school; middle to high school). It is also key to minimize disruptions to academic or psychological support services (and to eliminate gaps in treatment) during winter and summer breaks. Importantly, schools must recognize that the responsibility to request assistance with the child's academic and personal needs must not fall on the caregiver—who may not have the language skills or knowledge of how to approach educators, or whom may fear revealing their own undocumented status to others—nor on the student. As a helping institution, support for the student must be initiated by the school and should be a collaborative endeavor.

Measures to reduce interior enforcement

* Sanctuary policies

Protections for immigrant parents will positively impact US-born children. CBOs should continue to collaborate with policy makers to legislate an end to familial separation. In California, CBOs were instrumental in the passage of the California Values Act (SB 54) which bars law enforcement from using state resources, including personnel or facilities, to investigate or arrest anyone for federal immigration enforcement purposes. CBOs further strengthen SB 54 by urging law enforcement to exercise discretion and employ "cite and release" tactics in lieu of arrest. They note that this procedure allows law enforcement to protect residents in their city and thereby strengthens police-community relations. Opponents fear that persons with histories of violent offenses will receive a "free pass". However, most police arrests that result in transfers to ICE are for minor offenses, including personal drug use. Cite and release would thus significantly reduce the number of persons who have their information uploaded to a federal database and shared with ICE while still working with that individual to satisfy court orders via other non-confinement alternatives.

Universal representation should also be expanded. Through the advocacy of CBOs, cities across the nation have budgeted funds to cover legal counsel for immigrants in detention to obtain bond. This has allowed thousands of individuals to fight for their right to stay in the US free of cages. CBOs should continue to promote city and county-level universal representation for immigrants at the varying stages of their immigration cases.

* End ICE transfers

ICE's ability to carry out arrests relies on state and local law enforcement's cooperation to locate, apprehend, and detain non-citizens. These transfers are made possible via legislation such as IIRIRA and practices that criminalize non-serious and non-violent infractions including even arrests for traffic violations. County jails and state prisons have perpetuated crimmigration by fulfilling ICE detainer requests, which are no more than an ask to hold individuals beyond their release date so that ICE can conduct an interview to determine that person's immigration status. CBOs have criticized these collaborations as ruthless; they must continue to pressure sheriffs to not participate in these destructive practices. Ending ICE transfers would protect US-citizen children from the harms produced by parental detention and subsequent deportation, and, would facilitate pathways to legalization for their undocumented parents.

Measures to transform detention and deportation

- Alternatives to detention

    CBOs have actively urged courts to utilize release on recognizance instead of electronic monitoring and community supervision—two common alternatives that widen the net of state supervision and place a financial burden on non-citizens and their families. Electronic monitors are logistically difficult devices to manage (low battery life, uncomfortable and faulty); they are stigmatizing and pose as a barrier to finding employment. Community supervision has vastly expanded. In 2022, over 300,000 people were enrolled in the Intensive Supervision Appearance Program (ISAP), which requires in-person check-ins with an officer to ensure compliance and court appearance. Often, immigrants are presented with the option to download an app onto their mobile devices to check-in electronically. ISAP offers little transparency about exactly what data is collected and stored by private companies, or how that data may be managed long-term. Release on recognizance is a free, non-stigmatizing and non-dangerous alternative to detention that should be prioritized. CBOs can assist in identifying local services and constructing a strong reentry plan for the detainee, in line with the court's demands.
- Abolish immigration detention

    Detention is meant to serve as a temporary administrative hold while a person is processed for deportation. In reality, this type of confinement is experienced as incarceration with the same depravity of liberty and deplorable living conditions as those convicted of a criminal offense. In March of 2020, over 19,000 non-citizens were detained by ICE. In response to the global health crisis, by December of that year the number significantly dropped to 10,000 and fell again to under 4,600 by mid 2021—the lowest in decades. In California, the ACLU was victorious in mandating the Adelanto Detention Facility, one of the largest in the nation, to reduce its population to less than 250 persons, approximately a quarter of its maximum occupancy, in an effort to reduce the spread of the virus. CBOs across the nation have been influential in the termination of contracts with private companies that run these spaces of confinement. Trends of decarceration render arguments of immigrants as "flight risks" and "danger to society" unmerited. In the midst of the pandemic, the

US did not witness an increase in immigrants failing to appear in court—further signifying that detention is not a necessary apparatus. Abolishing detention would allow hundreds of thousands of families each year to remain together and protect the well-being of all members. CBOs should continue to work with policy makers to codify immigrant rights into federal law.

- Create pathways to legalization

  Ultimately, the power to protect US-citizen children with undocumented parents from the negative consequences of detention and deportation is to create opportunities for legalization. Approximately 11 million undocumented individuals currently reside in the country. In recent years immigration policy has become more restrictive, limiting opportunities for adjustment of status and deporting hundreds of thousands of individuals each year. Granting precarious legal statuses such as Deferred Action for Childhood Arrivals (DACA) and other forms of indeterminate relief, although beneficial, continue to perpetuate inequality among the undocumented population. These programs apply only to a small segment of the immigrant population, and are temporary, leaving the vast majority in legal limbo and vulnerable of falling out of status if such protections are revoked—as was attempted under the Trump administration. CBOs must continue to campaign for comprehensive immigration reform to remove the insecurity and fear of deportation prevalent among mixed-status families in the United States.

Notes

[1] Families whose members include persons with different citizenship or immigration statuses.
[2] Gulbas et al (2016).
[3] Vargas et al (2019).
[4] Golash-Boza (2019).
[5] Patler and Gonzalez (2021).
[6] Chaudry (2010).
[7] Dreby (2012).
[8] Rojas-Flores et al (2017).
[9] Gonzalez and Patler (2021).
[10] Cruz Nichols (2018).
[11] Amuedo-Dorantes and Lopez (2015).

Key resources

Amuedo-Dorantes, C. and Lopez, M. J. (2015) Falling through the cracks? Grade retention and school dropout among children of likely unauthorized immigrants. *American Economic Review*, 105(5): 598–603.

Chaudry, A., Capps, R., Pedroza, J. M., Castaneda, R. M., Santos, R., and Scott, M. M. (2010) Facing our future: children in the aftermath of immigration enforcement. *Urban Institute (NJ1)*. Available from: https://eric.ed.gov/?id=ED508226

Cruz Nichols, V., LeBrón, A. M., and Pedraza, F. I. (2018) Spillover effects: immigrant policing and government skepticism in matters of health for Latinos. *Public Administration Review*, 78(3): 432–43.

Dreby, J. (2012) The burden of deportation on children in Mexican immigrant families. *Journal of Marriage and Family*, 74(4): 829–45.

Golash-Boza, T. (2019) Punishment beyond the deportee: the collateral consequences of deportation. *American Behavioral Scientist*, 63(9): 1331–49.

Gonzalez, G. and Patler, C. (2021) The educational consequences of parental immigration detention. *Sociological Perspectives*, 64(2): 301–20.

Gulbas, L. E., Zayas, L. H., Yoon, H., Szlyk, H., Aguilar-Gaxiola, S., and Natera, G. (2016) Deportation experiences and depression among US citizen-children with undocumented Mexican parents. *Child: Care, Health and Development*, 42(2): 220–30.

Patler, C. and Gonzalez, G. (2021) Compounded vulnerability: the consequences of immigration detention for institutional attachment and system avoidance in mixed-immigration-status families. *Social Problems*, 68(4): 886–902.

Rojas-Flores, L., Clements, M. L., Hwang Koo, J., and London, J. (2017) Trauma and psychological distress in Latino citizen children following parental detention and deportation. *Psychological Trauma: Theory, Research, Practice, and Policy*, 9(3): 352.

Vargas, E. D., Juárez, M., Sanchez, G. R., and Livaudais, M. (2019) Latinos' connections to immigrants: how knowing a deportee impacts Latino health. *Journal of Ethnic and Migration Studies*, 45(15): 2971–88.

FIVE

News media and the crime coverage problem

Kristen M. Budd and Nazgol Ghandnoosh

The problem

News media have undoubtedly played a role in sustaining over 50 years of mass incarceration in the United States. It is hard to deny that news media— the public's primary source of crime information—have shaped public perceptions about who commits crime, the extent of the crime problem, and what we should do about it. Amidst a historic crime drop, the majority of Americans continued to believe that crime has been increasing in spite of voluminous evidence to the contrary.[1] Starting in the early 1990s, over the course of three decades, crime rates fell across the nation by roughly 50 percent.[2] While there was an increase in homicide rates during the social upheaval of the COVID-19 pandemic, these have now begun to decline and overall property crime rates have remained low.[3] Yet, counter to this reality, many Americans feel our criminal legal system is not tough enough on crime and continue to call for more policing.[4]

Contributing to public misperceptions about crime are news media headlines and corresponding stories that too often fail to offer context and nuance. Headlines such as "Ex-convict convicted in fatal shootings of 2 California women in 2016 near Las Vegas strip" and "Crimes committed by kids on the rise as expert warns harsher consequences needed: 'The penalties aren't scary'" run counter to what we know about adult and youth involvement in crime.[5] Contrary to common news media crime coverage, recidivism data tells us that individuals previously convicted of a crime of violence have an exceptionally low likelihood to later commit murder.[6] Arrests for youth aged 17 and under have fallen approximately 10 percent since 2000, representing only 6 percent of all arrests in 2020.[7] The deleterious effects of harsh punishment for youth have also been well documented.[8] While these headlines may garner public attention in an increasingly competitive media market, they do little to accurately portray crime and hamper the public's understanding of it.

In this chapter, we provide an overview of the research evidence highlighting the news media's role in spreading misinformation about crime, such as perpetuating racial stereotypes and crime myths, as well as its relationship to people's fear of crime. We then present a variety of recommendations to address crime coverage in the news media. These recommendations include ways to improve crime reporting and ways the public can better decipher crime news.

Research evidence

News media in the United States generally overdramatize and sensationalize crime. This includes the overreporting of crimes classified as violent.[9] "If it bleeds, it leads" is an old adage about news media coverage in America, particularly regarding homicide, even though crimes classified as non-violent are much more prevalent (for example, property crimes). News media also contribute to either generating or reinforcing crime myths, such as exaggerating people of color's level of involvement in crime. The following research evidence illustrates how many news outlets perpetuate misinformation about crime.

News media and race and ethnicity

- Television news programs and newspapers over-represent people of color as crime suspects and Whites as crime victims. Black and Latinx suspects are also more likely than Whites to be presented in a non-individualized and threatening way—unnamed and in police custody. Such skewed coverage contributes to the public's association of crime with people of color and perpetuates racial stereotypes about the propensity for criminal behavior.[10] The disproportionate coverage of White crime victims also understates people of color's level of victimization by crime.
- Neighborhood racial composition plays a role in the newsworthiness of homicide victimizations, or the amount of coverage received. A study of Chicago homicides found that victims killed in predominantly Black neighborhoods received less news coverage than those killed in predominantly White neighborhoods, even after accounting for victim race and the rate of homicides in the neighborhoods.[11] Moreover, those killed in predominantly Black or Latinx neighborhoods were less likely to be discussed as complex, multidimensional people.

News media and the immigration-crime nexus

- Many news media outlets continue to perpetuate myths and stereotypes about immigrants' level of involvement in crime. Research analyzing over 2,000 stories published in ten high-circulation national papers found that the most prominent media frame about immigration and crime was the criminogenic frame (50 percent of the news articles). This frame described immigrants themselves as being particularly crime prone, described crime incidents involving a foreign-born person, or linked immigration to higher rates of crimes in communities.[12] This frame became more prominent in the narratives over the study's time frame (1990–2013). This narrative is counter to the extensive body of empirical evidence that finds immigrants are less likely to commit crime than their US-born counterparts.[13]

News media and public fear

• There is a relationship between news media consumption and people's level of fear of crime. Research has consistently found that consuming higher levels of television news and non-fictional crime programming is associated with a greater fear of crime. Local news effects—TV news coverage about where you live versus national coverage—have been shown to have a stronger relationship to the level of fear of crime, particularly if one lives in a high crime area or was a recent victim of crime.[14]

Recommendations and solutions

Because news media are a critical component informing the public about crime and justice issues, reporters and editors should strive for accuracy and context and individuals should aim to be critical consumers of media content. To address news media coverage's role in shaping public perceptions of crime and policy responses to crime, we offer two sets of recommendations. Our first set of recommendations describes how to reformulate and improve news media coverage to better relay factual information about crime and crime policy. The second set of recommendations provides guidance to community members so that they become critical consumers of crime and justice information whether it be from news media outlets or other media channels.

Recommendations to improve crime coverage

• Situate crime stories, and proposed solutions, within their broader historical and geographic context

Patterns of crime and crime rates change over time—20-year versus 1-year trends—and vary by geographic location—by state and within states. They are influenced by disruptions in social and economic life (such as the COVID-19 pandemic). While covering national crime trends from year-to-year provides relevant information, it excludes historical comparisons as well as omits local context. Well-framed stories about crime increases should consider the following questions: Is the shift unique to one form of crime and is it attributable to a change in crime reporting or recording? How do changes in crime rates compare to historical peaks and lows, and how does it compare with trends in other jurisdictions? If crime rates increased in several jurisdictions, this should inspire skepticism that a particular local reform is to blame. Journalists should seek out evidence and engage in critical inquiry before attributing crime upticks to a failure of policy.

- Recognize and discuss the limited and declining role of crimes committed by youth

    Once again, there are many alarmist narratives about youth involvement in crime, even though many crimes in the United States are the result of adults engaging in law-breaking behavior. This echoes past coverage of the alleged youth "super predators." Although this myth was debunked, the intersection of political rhetoric, media messaging, and public fear created a long-lasting and severely detrimental response to youth involvement in crime (such as sending youth through the adult court system). The evidence does not support recent media messaging of youth-driven increases in crime rates. News media should avoid sensationalizing youth crime. They should ask—does our coverage over-represent youth relative to adult crime? Over-representation of youth crime continues to perpetuate youth crime myths and trigger punitive responses that cause great harm.

- Conduct a racial equity audit on the quantity and quality of crime coverage

    As discussed in the research evidence section, crime coverage skews in who it shows committing crime (such as Black males) and who it shows being victimized by crime (such as White females). Moreover, coverage of crime incidents involving people of color fails to capture the complexity of individuals by noting, for example, their family and community roles. News media outlets should conduct audits of how their news coverage captures the accuracy of their market's crime and victimization rates. They should continuously audit, and correct biased coverage of how they present individuals. Media outlets should also strive to have diverse representation not only in their news coverage, but also in their newsrooms.

- Use non-stigmatizing, person-first language in crime news coverage

    News media must transition to using first-person language (for example, "a person who broke the law," "an incarcerated person," "a person with a prior conviction") in their reporting. Research has documented the dehumanizing effects and stigma that result from the negative labels such as those used to describe people who are involved in the criminal legal system (for example, "murderer," "prisoner," "ex-convict"). Such terms dehumanize individuals and create dichotomies of "us" versus "them." These labels are powerful. They influence public perceptions and contribute to the public support for harsh penalties and a variety of community social control mechanisms (such as public internet disclosure for certain sex crime convictions, or housing restrictions).[15]

• Increase the number of success stories that document the progress resulting from criminal legal reforms

"On criminal justice, don't just focus on bad news. We ignore progress at our peril."[16] Crime news tends to focus on the sensational, and often the negative, while ignoring the success stories that do result from criminal legal reforms. For example, Washington, DC has seen success as a result of its second-look law, which permits DC residents who have served at least 15 years for crimes they committed before their 25th birthday to petition for resentencing. Here is one headline documenting the benefits of this reform: "Halim Flowers was given two life sentences at 17. Now, his art is shown worldwide."[17] News media should increase the quantity and quality of crime and justice news that highlights the success of criminal legal reforms, including profiles of those impacted by these reforms. Such coverage provides much needed balance for community members given that they use crime news media for much of their knowledge.

Recommendations for consumers of news media

In the United States, we are saturated with news media coverage, whether this is traditional media (televised coverage or print) or new media (social media outlets like Facebook, Instagram, and TikTok). Next we provide questions consumers should ask when assessing and evaluating coverage on crime and justice. These recommendations stem from scholarly work and news media literacy tactics.

• For news media reporting, we encourage consumers to ask four critical questions: Who authored or created this news piece? Why was this news piece created? Is it credible? Is it biased?

These four questions can help consumers evaluate and judge information they are receiving through various news media outlets. Was it created by a journalist who included impartial experts and factual data? Was it created to partially support one perspective or to present a complete picture? There are also tools available online to help news media consumers to assess the ideological stance and potential bias of news outlets. For example, Vanessa Otero, J.D., founder of Ad Fontes Media, created "The Media Bias Chart." It rates news sources, which includes online and print newspaper articles, podcasts, and TV shows, on two characteristics: reliability and bias. Currently on the 11th iteration, it rates bias from "most extreme" left to middle to "most extreme" right as well as the news value and reliability (for example, "thorough fact reporting/ fact-dense analysis" versus "contains inaccurate/fabricated information").

While not directly related to crime news, we are also living in an era of crime-based reality programming, crime dramas, and docuseries. It is important to keep at the forefront that these shows were created for entertainment. They were not created to be a source of facts about crime. Such shows offer a particular version of policing, of individuals involved in criminal behavior or victimized by it, and the response of the criminal legal system. More often than not, such portrayals do not reflect the crime statistics in the localities in which they are cast and are not representative of typical criminal justice encounters.[18]

- For crime statistics and polling on criminal legal issues that are presented in the news media, ask three critical questions: Who created this statistic? How was this statistic created? Why was the statistic created?[19]

  Crime statistics and the presentation of crime data are social creations. People design polls—determining question wording, answer choices, and sampling strategy—as well as analyze the data. We should never forget there is a human element and organizational context to statistical creation. As for who created the statistic, was it a federal agency (such as the Bureau of Justice Statistics)? Was it a news media outlet? Was it a partisan or non-partisan non-profit or think tank? Does the source tell the consumer how the statistic was created? Was the statistic created using a random sample of Americans or a non-random door-to-door survey? Last, why was the statistic created? Was it created for factual knowledge? Was it created to persuade? Such inquisitive questions can help consumers figure out why these numbers are being used and how the numbers provide meaning to the news media's messaging.

- Seek out alternative forms of news media and dig deeper into crime and justice issues

  Non-profit organizations such as The Marshall Project provide rigorous coverage of crime and crime policies. News consumers can access their coverage freely online and also sign up for their newsletters. Organizations including The Sentencing Project, where both authors work, produce broadly accessible reports relevant to prominent debates about crime and crime policy. Other research-oriented non-profit organizations, including the Urban Institute, the Brennan Center, Vera Institute of Justice, and the Council on Criminal Justice, also produce accessible reports that offer a chance to dig deeper into crime and criminal legal issues and develop a knowledge base from which to contextualize news media coverage.

Recommendations for scholars

- Scholars should increase their engagement with the news media in order to infuse their expert knowledge into reporting streams.

Scholars, as experts in their field, should be encouraged to engage with the news media (such as via professional organizations or their institutions). They have the opportunity to both inform and provide feedback when there is poor coverage on crime and criminal legal issues. They can also use other avenues, such as Op-Eds, Letters to the Editor, and social media, to infuse their expert knowledge into news media and public discourse. Institutions of higher education and professional organizations can provide support to engage in such interactions by facilitating training in Op-Ed writing, pitching stories to the news media, responding to news media requests, and by rewarding such public engagement. Additionally, organizations such as the Scholars Strategy Network work to assist scholars in translating their research for public consumption.

Notes

[1] Brenan, M. (2022) Record-high 56% in U.S. perceive local crime has increased. Gallup. Available from: https://news.gallup.com/poll/404048/record-high-perceive-local-crime-increased.aspx; Lopez, G. (2016) Americans don't know crime has plummeted. In fact, they think it's gone up. *Vox*, [online] October 10. Available from: https://www.vox.com/policy-and-politics/2016/10/10/13226264/us-crime-rate-poll

[2] Rosenfeld, R., Boxerman, B., and Lopez. E. (2023) Pandemic, social unrest, and crime in U.S. Cities: Year-end 2022 update. Council on Criminal Justice. Available from: https://counciloncj.org/pandemic-social-unrest-and-crime-in-u-s-cities-year-end-2022-update/

[3] The latest 2022 release of FBI Crime in the Nation Statistics documented a roughly 7 percent annual increase in property crime, which was mostly driven by the rise in motor vehicle thefts (+11 percent) and larceny theft (+8 percent). Burglaries/breaking and entering remained flat. These statistics can be found on the Federal Bureau of Investigation's Crime Data Explorer (https://cde.ucr.cjis.gov/LATEST/webapp/#/pages/home).

[4] Brenan, M. (2023) Americans more critical of U.S. criminal justice system. Gallup. Available from: https://news.gallup.com/poll/544439/americans-critical-criminal-justice-system.aspx

[5] Associated Press (2023) Ex-convict convicted in fatal shootings of 2 California women in 2016 near Las Vegas strip. Fox News, [online] October 11. Available from: https://www.foxnews.com/us/ex-convict-convicted-fatal-shootings-2-california-women-2016-near-las-vegas-strip; Casiano, L. (2022) Crimes committed by kids on the rise as expert warns harsher consequences needed: 'The penalties aren't scary.' Fox News, [online] October 27. Available from: https://www.foxnews.com/us/crimes-committed-kids-rise-expert-warns-harsher-consequences-needed

[6] Durose, M., R., Cooper, A. D., and Snyder, H. N. (2014) Recidivism of prisoners released in 30 states in 2005: Patterns from 2005 to 2010. Bureau of Justice Statistics. Available from: https://bjs.ojp.gov/content/pub/pdf/rprts05p0510.pdf

[7] OJJDP (2022) Trend in percent of arrests by age group for all offenses. *OJJDP Statistical Briefing Book*. Available from: https://www.ojjdp.gov/ojstatbb/crime/ucr_trend.asp?table_in=1

[8] Mendel, R. (2023) Why youth incarceration fails: an updated review of the evidence. The Sentencing Project. Available from: https://www.sentencingproject.org/reports/why-youth-incarceration-fails-an-updated-review-of-the-evidence/

[9] See, for example, O'Hear, M. (2020) Violent crime and media coverage in one city: a statistical snapshot. *Marquette Law Review*, 103(3): 1007–33.

[10] Ghandnoosh, N. (2014) Race and punishment: Racial perceptions of crime and support for punitive policies. The Sentencing Project. Available from: https://www.sentencing project.org/app/uploads/2022/08/Race-and-Punishment.pdf

[11] White, K., Stuart, F., and Morrissey, S. L. (2021) Whose lives matter? Race, space, and the devaluation of homicide victims in minority communities. *Sociology of Race and Ethnicity*, 7(3): 333–49.

[12] Harris, C. T. and Gruenewald, J. (2020) News media trends in the framing of immigration and crime, 1990–2013. *Social Problems*, 67(3): 452–70.

[13] Ghandnoosh, N. and Rovner, J. (2017) Immigration and public safety. The Sentencing Project. Available from: http://www.sentencingproject.org/wp-content/uploads/2017/03/Immigration-and-Public-Safety.pdf

[14] See, for example, Chiricos, T., Eschholz, S., and Gertz, M. (1997) Crime, news and fear of crime: toward an identification of audience effects. *Social Problems*, 44(3): 342–57; Chiricos, T., Padgett, K., and Gertz, M. (2000) Fear, TV news, and the reality of crime. *Criminology*, 38(3), 755–86; Eschholz, S., Chiricos, T., Gertz, M., Problems, S., and August, N. (2003). Television and fear of crime: program types, audience traits, and the mediating effect of perceived neighborhood composition. *Social Problems*, 50(3): 395–415.

[15] See, for example, Harris, A. J. and Socia, K. M. (2016) What's in a name? Evaluating the effects of the 'sex offender' label on public opinions and beliefs. *Sexual Abuse*, 28(7): 660–78.

[16] Gelb, A. (2023) On criminal justice, don't just focus on bad news. We ignore progress at our peril. *USA Today*, [online] September 23. Available from: https://www.usatoday.com/story/opinion/voices/2023/09/23/crime-statistics-progress-arrests-incarceration-homicide-murder/70867322007/

[17] Williams, E. C. (2021) Halim Flowers was given two life sentences at 17. Now, his art is shown worldwide. NPR, [online] December 3. Available from: https://www.npr.org/local/305/2021/12/03/1061183998/halim-flowers-was-given-two-life-sentences-at-17-now-his-art-is-shown-worldwide

[18] See, for example, Britto, S., Hughes, T., Saltzman, K., and Stroh, C. (2007) Does 'special' mean young, white, and female? Deconstructing the meaning of 'special' in Law & Order: Special Victims Unit. *Journal of Criminal Justice and Popular Culture*, 14(1): 39–57.

[19] Best, J. (2012). *Damned Lies and Statistics: Untangling Numbers from the Media, Politicians, and Activists*. University of California Press.

Key resources

Best, J. (2012) *Damned Lies and Statistics: Untangling Numbers from The Media, Politicians, and Activists*. University of California Press.

Bogert, C. and Hancock, L. (2020) Analysis: How the media created a 'superpredator' myth that harmed a generation of Black youth. NBC News, [online] November 20. Available from: https://www.nbcnews.com/news/us-news/analysis-how-media-created-superpredator-myth-harmed-generation-black-youth-n1248101

Dorfman, L. and Schiraldi, V. (2001) *Off Balance: Youth, Race, & Crime in The News*. Youth Law Center. Available from: https://www.bmsg.org/wp-content/uploads/2001/04/bmsg_other_publication_off_balance.pdf

Ghandnoosh, N. (2022) *Media Guide: 10 Crime Coverage Dos and Don'ts*. The Sentencing Project. Available from: https://www.sentencingproject.org/app/uploads/2022/08/10-Crime-Coverage-Dos-and-Donts.pdf

McBride, K. (2023) Local newsrooms want to stop sensationalizing crime, but it's hard. Pynter. Available from: https://www.poynter.org/ethics-trust/2023/journalists-if-it-bleeds-it-leads-accountability-reporting/#:~:text=The%20first%20step%20is%20to,to%20the%20modest%20traffic%20spikes

Otero, V. (2023) *The Media Bias Chart*, Version 11.0. Available from: https://adfontesmedia.com/interactive-media-bias-chart/?utm_source=LI_VO81523

Shaw, M. (2017) Photos reveal media's softer tone on opioid crisis. *Columbia Journalism Review*. Available from: https://www.cjr.org/criticism/opioid-crisis-photos.php?link

Stone-Mediatore, S. (n.d.) Tough questions for tough-on-crime policies. Ohio Wesleyan University. Available from: https://www.owu.edu/news-media/from-our-perspective/tough-questions-for-tough-on-crime-policies/

PART II

Education

SIX

Caught in the crossfire: K-12 education and anti-CRT measures

Ashley N. Gwathney and Charity Anderson

The problem

Few topics in education have dominated the news since 2021 as much as efforts to ban critical race theory (CRT) from public schools in the United States. The larger problem is the widespread effort to impede public education, stifling students' opportunities to think critically about our nation's history and denying them their right to a complete education. In September 2020, after protests over the police killing of George Floyd prompted new conversations about structural racism in the US, the Trump administration issued a memo to federal agencies directing them to identify and cancel any staff trainings that focused on CRT or "White privilege." Weeks later, President Trump issued Executive Order 13950, prohibiting federal agencies and recipients of federal funding from teaching "divisive concepts," including the idea that the US is "fundamentally racist or sexist." Trump's focus on CRT likely originated with a 2020 Fox News interview of Christopher F. Rufo, a conservative scholar, who warned of the "cult indoctrination" of CRT and the "danger and destruction it can wreak"; Rufo helped draft the Executive Order.

Conservative think tanks, thought leaders, media figures, and politicians operationalized and conflated "divisive concepts" to mean "CRT"—a college-level analytical framework rarely taught in K-12 schools that examines how race and racism intersect with other forms of social identity, power, and oppression. The theory, which emerged in the mid-1980s in American law schools, holds that racism is not simply expressed on a microlevel but, rather, is deeply rooted in the nation's laws, policies, regulations, and institutions (such as the criminal justice system, education system, labor market, housing market, and healthcare system).

Although the Order was rescinded by President Biden on his first day in office, its impact on K-12 education was already well underway: As of December 2022, all states except Delaware have introduced anti-CRT legislation that, in practice, seeks to ban books, vet teaching practices, and restrict curricula in American history, civics, and government, and 28 states have adopted measures that ban the teaching of race and racism, affecting over 22 million public school children—almost half of the country's 50.8 million public school students.[1] The National Council for Social Studies criticized this growing trend, stating, "CRT has been used ... to ban the teaching of such concepts as race, racism, White supremacy, equity, justice, and social-emotional learning, as well as to limit the teaching of content such as slavery, Black history, women's suffrage, LGBTQI issues, and civil rights." Ironically, anti-CRT legislation confirms that racism is indeed embedded in our laws and systems.

While the rampant misuse of the term "CRT" is certainly a concern, and those waging anti-CRT campaigns rarely engage with the academic substance of the theory, preparing students for civic engagement by teaching complete history is critical, but anti-CRT measures, which often take the form of book bans and curriculum gag orders, make it impossible for every child to receive a high-quality and age-appropriate education by dictating whose history, identities, and voices should be heard. What's more, hampering inquiry refutes the national reckoning on race propelled by the Black Lives Matter movement and undermines students' development of knowledge, self-reflection, and free speech, raising broader concerns about the erosion of constitutional rights and democratic principles in our country.[2] Laws prohibiting educators or curricula from mentioning race and/or racism censor classroom discussion and provide cover for those who are uncomfortable with the history of racism in the US. This chapter shares the best available knowledge about anti-CRT measures in public education and provides recommendations for elected officials, policy makers, community members, and the public.

Research evidence

Despite the short life of Executive Order 13950—signed, enjoined, and revoked in roughly 4 months—its impact continues to be felt. The anti-CRT campaign that accompanied the Order is not a fringe movement but, instead, is one that is pervasive and coordinated, with serious implications for our nation's public school students. Researchers at UCLA's School of Law track anti-CRT legislation, executive orders, state attorney general letters, and statements by governors and local school board officials as part of the Tracking Project. The Project's most recent report, "Tracking the Attack on Critical Race Theory," found that between January 1, 2021, and December 31, 2022, policy makers at federal, state, and local levels introduced 563 anti-CRT measures, and nearly half—241—were adopted. The language from the Order continues to live on in local and state legislation. Nearly half of the measures introduced by lawmakers feature borrowed wording, such as references to "divisive concepts," from the now-repealed Order.

According to the report, anti-CRT measures were overwhelmingly, although not entirely, aimed at teaching in public schools: over 90 percent of the measures targeted K-12 institutions. Among the measures aimed at public schools, 76 percent restrict curricula, 65 percent surveil classroom teaching, and 28 percent allow parents to submit allegations of "indoctrination" through tip-lines.[3] In terms of content, measures specifically targeting CRT and the *New York Times'* "1619 Project," a long-form, multimedia journalism project that reframes America's origin story around the legacy of slavery, were the most likely to be adopted or enacted after introduction.

The current anti-CRT laws and rules vary in scope and content, but two things are clear: they do not have anything to do with actual CRT, and their language bears a close resemblance to that of Executive Order 13950. In Alabama, the House approved a 2022 bill restricting the teaching of race and history and forbidding teaching a list of "divisive concepts," including the idea that "this state or the United States is inherently racist or sexist." Similarly, Arizona's signed bill prohibits the teaching of unconscious bias or responsibility for historic acts of racism. Tennessee's signed bill withholds funding from schools if teachers connect events to institutional racism. But the campaign against CRT and antiracist teaching, training, and research is not limited to traditionally conservative states. In California, for example, the Placentia-Yorba Linda Unified School District, about 30 miles from Los Angeles, enacted a resolution that banned CRT and instead advanced a colorblind ideology of "see[ing] one another as humans first," which ignores the pervasiveness of racism within American society. In Colorado, 100 percent of introduced local school board anti-CRT measures have been enacted, and Tracking Project data show that two of Colorado's measures were passed in districts where anti-CRT school board candidates were funded, endorsed, and elected to their positions with the support of an anti-CRT political action committee (PAC). New Jersey represents a noteworthy divergence from the prevailing anti-CRT trends. Unlike Arkansas, Florida, and Texas, which have all enacted statewide bans on teaching AP African American History in secondary schools, New Jersey has expanded access from one school to 26 schools for the 2023–24 school year. The deliberate departure signals an active push against the growing casualties of anti-CRT movements.

Still, the anti-CRT movement is far from over and shows no signs of slowing down. In fact, during the first 3 months of 2023, UCLA researchers tracked at least 50 new anti-CRT bills and expect to see more activity through the 2024 presidential election cycle as lawmakers craft the next wave of laws and policies based on the first generation of anti-CRT measures already codified into law and policy. This is an important development to note because anti-CRT measures directly impact K-12 students, who make up the most racially, ethnically, and gender-diverse population in the nation. Our nation is rapidly aging, and future generations need to know how and why America's current racial and ethnic divides came into being. This will put them in a position to offer solutions that will contribute to both their own well-being and that of the older generations who will become increasingly dependent on them.

Orchestrated anti-CRT efforts deprive students of opportunities to see themselves and others and narrow the range of viewpoints and ideas accessible in schools.[4] Educational research shows that navigating controversial issues in classrooms, critically addressing difficult histories, and evidence-based inquiry into public issues are key to developing young people's capacity for civic reasoning and discourse.[5] Research also shows that being educated about racism leads children to be more equity-driven. On the surface, anti-CRT measures may appear to be a focused attack on content, but the policies actually deny students the substance and skills required for informed democratic citizenship, which includes engaging with multiple points of view and critically analyzing information.

Recommendations and solutions

In some instances, some of the most extreme and misguided provisions of these measures have been rejected by legislators and governors. The arguments used to defeat these bills—including that they compound the already difficult work of teachers, deny students' rights, override the wishes of most parents, put youth at risk, and distract from the true purpose of schools—are powerful ones that call for greater amplification and recognition.

CRT has been under attack since 2020, and the movement has mutated, broadened in scope, and grown more extreme over time. As such, it is unlikely that any across-the-board strategy could counter the extent of the problematic attacks across the US. Such anti-democratic actions are best countered not through academic debate but through political mobilization and democratic engagement. Thus, resistance should account for a myriad of institutional actors, including media outlets, legislative measures, legal efforts, and social activism. The following recommendations offer a solution-focused framework to address the challenges of anti-CRT measures.

Media actions

- Critical media literacy is key. While many media organizations have produced strong programming about CRT and the orchestrated controversy surrounding it, many have let evidence-free arguments slide. What passes for in-depth coverage often tends toward generalized talking points that journalists do not challenge or probe. The media can dig deeper into arguments for and against anti-CRT measures and can reframe the debate around anti-CRT campaigns to include messaging that acknowledges race and racism as a shared stake of Americans of all racial backgrounds and provide specific examples of solutions.[6]

Political actions

- While conservatives are united around anti-CRT rhetoric, moderates and liberals have not coalesced in an opposition campaign. Rather than dismissing manufactured concerns over CRT as fake, political moderates and liberals should embrace the teaching of America's racial history and make a strong, affirmative case for why it matters for American values of fairness, equality, and justice. They can then focus on articulating how attacks on CRT are meant to divide people of all races who otherwise share interests. Rather than dismissing these attacks as isolated incidents, they should mount a sustained and coherent campaign to argue for the truthful teaching of American history and current events that acknowledges the reality of race, racism, and inequality. In fact, one of the architects of CRT, Kimberlé Crenshaw, has argued that talking about systemic racial inequality in America's past and present is actually an act of patriotism.
- Legislators should ensure that accountability systems are in place for protecting students' rights and that all students are receiving a quality education. Failure to protect students' rights to a quality of education that teaches complete and accurate American history, literature, civics, and government is a violation of the Department of Education's mission to "promote student achievement and preparation for global competitiveness by fostering educational excellence and ensuring equal access." The Department must continue to monitor the state and local landscape of school curricula on American history, as well as state actions on book banning, and offer technical guidance to schools that seek to implement more inclusive strategies or other policies ensuring that school districts are not violating students' First Amendment rights.

Legal actions

- There are consequences for allowing anti-CRT laws to remain on the books. Educators who violate an anti-CRT law can face disciplinary action or lose their teaching license. Schools and districts can be sued, lose their accreditation, or lose state funding. The decision of whether to challenge anti-CRT laws in court is still a difficult one, but framing anti-CRT measures as simply political theater, or dismissing them because CRT is not taught in K-12 schools, may lead advocates to forego litigating anti-CRT laws for the wrong reasons. The American Civil Liberties Union is currently filing lawsuits on behalf of students, teachers, and college professors, arguing that anti-CRT measures violate students' First Amendment rights and are so vaguely written that teachers and students can't understand what is forbidden and what is allowed. Legal precedent can guide states in enacting laws and policies that explicitly safeguard intellectual freedom and set forth clear guidelines for addressing anti-CRT measures through book bans, teaching surveillance, and ideological vetting of students and staff.[7]

Policies

- Allocation of funds to promote community engagement and awareness of academic freedom can be implemented at the state and local levels. Legislators and their constituents, including parents and school board members, can advocate for measures that require schools to include a variety of perspectives, including those that address historical events, social issues, and marginalized communities.
- State Education Agencies (SEAs) can also play a crucial role in upholding students' First Amendment rights by allocating funding for school-based programs to provide teacher, administrator, and librarian training on culturally responsive practices and the importance of exposing students to various perspectives. SEAs can also include clear guidelines for addressing challenges to books and curricular materials along with allocation of funding to diversify curriculum, faculty, and staff.[8]
- School officials have a constitutional duty to safeguard students' rights and freedoms, ensuring that curriculum decisions are made without bias or attempting to promote political or religious ideologies.[9] They can support stakeholders in informed decision-making that benefits students of all backgrounds and the education system as a whole.[10]
- Proactive, *anti*-anti-CRT efforts can happen at both the state and local levels. For example, the Washington State Legislature passed S.B. 5044—signed into law May 5, 2021—a bill "[r]elating to equity, cultural competency, and dismantling institutional racism in the public school system," which called for collaboration between the state school directors' association and the state professional educator standards board. As a team, they were to, in part, "develop trainings to incorporate cultural competency standards" into state teaching standards and practices.

Social actions

- Anti-CRT measures are an organized effort to uphold structural inequities by suppressing accurate information about history, blocking access to democratic participation, and undermining public schooling.

Stakeholders, such as parents, teachers, and students, can proactively engage in conversations with school administrators, district officials, and policy makers to advocate for clear policies that protect academic freedom in schools and library systems.[11]

- When Americans call their legislators, join school boards, or utilize social media platforms to share their concerns about education, they are exercising the right to make their voices heard—a right that is central to the civic engagement process.

- School districts and parent-teacher organizations can generate public campaigns on the benefits of attending and participating in local school board meetings, particularly ones that aim to remove or restrict curricula and/or books.[12] The Honest Education Action and Leadership (H.E.A.L.) Together initiative, a partnership with New York University's Metropolitan Center for Research and Equity and the Transformation of Schools, the Schott Foundation for Public Education, the National Education Association, and others, offers tools and trainings for students, parents, and educators to organize for educational equity.

Notes

[1] Alexander et al (2023).

[2] López et al (2022).

[3] Alexander et al (2023).

[4] Meehan, K. and Friedman, J. (2023) Banned in the USA: State laws supercharge book suppression in schools. Report for Pen America. Available from: https://pen.org/report/banned-in-the-usa-state-laws-supercharge-book-suppression-in-schools/

[5] National Center for Institutional Diversity. (2023). Spark Series: Miseducating the Public. https://lsa.umich.edu/ncid/news-events/all-news/spark/series-essays/spark-series-miseducating-the-public.html

[6] Morgan (2022), see note 1.

[7] Morgan (2022), see note 1.

[8] National Coalition Against Censorship (2023a).

[9] National Coalition Against Censorship (2023b) The first amendment in schools. Available from: https://ncac.org/resource/first-amendment-in-school

[10] Morgan (2022), see note 1.

[11] National Coalition Against Censorship (2023a).

[12] ALA (2023).

Key resources

Alexander, T., Clark, L. B., Reinhard, K., and Zatz, N. (2023) Tracking the attack on Critical Race Theory. CRT Forward. Available from: https://crtforward.law.ucla.edu/wpcontent/uploads/2023/04/UCLA-Law_CRT-Report_Final.pdf

American Library Association (ALA) (2023) *Unite Against Book Bans Toolkit*. Available from: https://uniteagainstbookbans.org/wp-content/uploads/2023/02/UABB-Toolkit-2-17-2023.pdf

Harris, E. A. and Alter, A. (2022) A fast-growing network of conservative groups is fueling a surge in book Bans. *The New York Times*, [online] December 12. Available from: https://www.nytimes.com/2022/12/12/books/book-bans-libraries.html

Knox, L. (2023) Anti-CRT measures exploded last year, report finds. Available from: https://www.insidehighered.com/quicktakes/2023/04/07/anti-crt-measures-exploded-last-year-report-finds

López, F., Molnar, A., Johnson, R., Patterson, A., Ward, L., and Kumashiro, K. (2022) Understanding the attacks on Critical Race Theory. National Education Policy Center. Available from: https://nepc.colorado.edu/publication/crt

Morgan, H. (2022). Resisting the movement to ban Critical Race Theory from schools. *The Clearing House*, 95(1): 35–41.

National Center for Institutional Diversity (2023) *Spark Series: Miseducating the Public.* University of Michigan. Available from: https://lsa.umich.edu/ncid/news-events/all-news/spark/series-essays/spark-series-miseducating-the-public.html

National Coalition Against Censorship (2023a) Kids Rights to Read Action Kit. Available from: https://ncac.org/wp-content/uploads/2022/07/KRRP-Action-Kit-2022.pdf

National Education Association (2021) *Racial Justice in Education Framework.* Available from: https://www.nea.org/resource-library/racial-justice-education-framework

U.S. Department of Education (2022) *2022 Agency Equity Plan Related to Executive Order 13985.* Available from: https://www2.ed.gov/documents/equity/2022-equity-plan.pdf

Inequality in the experiential core: using pathways to understand and improve college students' journeys

Blake R. Silver and Monique H. Harrison

The problem

As we approach the 2024 elections, and in the wake of recent Supreme Court decisions on college admissions and student debt relief, national conversations have once again focused on college access and affordability. The elimination of affirmative action in college admissions, struggles to find policy solutions for exorbitant student debt, and concerns about inadequate preparation in high school literacy and math make an emphasis on these topics inevitable and important. Though these are crucial conversations, a focus on inequality in college access risks overlooking the inequalities that emerge once students arrive on campus. For those who gain admissions and manage to pay tuition, inequality does not stop at matriculation.

While scholars of higher education have long been cognizant of the complex role higher education can play in social mobility and social reproduction, common frameworks for understanding higher education have centered on questions of inputs and outcomes. For instance, a focus on "pipelines" to, through, and beyond higher education aligns with tendencies to emphasize college enrollment, retention, and completion. Over the past decade, however, scholars and practitioners alike have begun emphasizing the importance of college student experiences.

Emerging research illuminates the complexity of students' experiences on campus—from examining the elective curriculum, in which students have almost limitless course options, to the extracurricular components of student life (clubs, sports, jobs, and so on). This work examines the impact of students' experiences on stratification, explaining how inequalities persist between students who are advantaged or marginalized on the basis of race, ethnicity, social class, gender, sexual orientation, immigration, and a host of other sociodemographic characteristics. This chapter explores what we are learning in this regard through research focused on 4-year colleges and universities with attention to solutions that can combat inequality.

We propose that attention be paid both to research that centers students' curricular journeys as well as work that studies the social, extracurricular, and pre-professional opportunities that contribute to undergraduate "pathways," a framing concept that moves away from pipeline metaphors and emphasizes looking closely at students' iterative decision-making and experiences to understand and improve their educational journeys.[1] We use the pathways framework to examine how students navigate the broad array of curricular and extracurricular opportunities; we propose specific ways to identify and address inequality within higher education.

Research evidence

Inequality in college student experiences

In their review of the literature on student experiences in college, Richard Arum and colleagues described the contours of inequality in undergraduate student experiences.[2] Early sociological research on higher education focused primarily on issues of access and outcomes, relying mainly on broad quantitative descriptions of enrollment, retention, graduation, and career attainment. But the turn of the 21st century saw new interest in the "black box" or "experiential core" of higher education as scholars worked to better understand what happens between the moments of college enrollment and graduation.[3]

Research has called attention to the often taken-for-granted structure of the elective curriculum, which provides some general requirements, but largely allows for student discretion and empowers them to tailor their own college experience. The freedom to choose is a cherished value in US higher education but can create the circumstances that reproduce inequality and the potential for stalled progress.[4] How students make decisions about courses and extracurricular activities, how their decision processes changes over time, and the impacts of early decisions have yet to be fully understood.

Some research has examined student experiences and developed important insights about the prevalence and dimensions of inequality on college campuses. This inequality emerges in students' access to information and opportunities, perceptions of campus climate and feelings of belonging, and daily interactions with peers, faculty, and administration. Research demonstrates, for instance, that socioeconomic inequality in students' familiarity with higher education—what many scholars refer to as "college knowledge"—leads to disparities in students' capacities to anticipate and respond to faculty expectations, thereby shaping academic success. These inequalities in students' familiarity navigating college opportunities correspond with disparities in participation in high impact learning experiences like undergraduate research, study abroad, and internships. For example, while student engagement in internship opportunities has increased over recent decades, low-income students and first-generation students remain less likely to take part in these experiences than their higher-income, continuing-generation peers.[5] Moreover, chilly campus and classroom climates can undermine student success for women and students of color, especially in settings where they remain under-represented such as science, technology, engineering, and math (STEM) fields.

While earlier exploration of such inequality focused largely on disparities by socioeconomic status, race/ethnicity, or gender, emerging work relies more directly on intersectional frameworks that account for the mutual constitution of these dimensions of lived experience. Patricia Hill Collins and Semra Bilge note, "Intersectionality is a way of understanding and analyzing the complexity in the world, in people, and in human experiences." They advocate for understanding social phenomena "as being shaped not by a single axis of social division, be it race or gender or class, but by many axes that work together and influence each other."[6]

Scholars taking up this call show how an intersectional lens exposes inequalities in students' experiences of higher education that previously have been neglected or misunderstood. Studies find that Black women, for example, have experiences on college campuses that differ in important ways from the experiences of Black men as well as from White women.[7] Analyses that explored race or gender separately would miss these experiential differences. Being able to account for intersectional student experiences— and related questions of power and influence—opens up new possibilities for understanding inequality across students' educational journeys, a project that requires exploring the burgeoning research on undergraduate educational pathways.

Undergraduate pathways

The concept of undergraduate pathways made its way to the sociology of education in a piecemeal fashion. Though scholars came to acknowledge the importance of studying student experiences, few initially thought about these experiences in sequential or cumulative ways. That began to change with the emergence of longitudinal ethnographic work and new computational methods for quantitatively examining students' sequential and often dependent patterns of enrollment. Drawing from their multi-year study of 53 college women who began their journeys on the same first-year residence hall floor, Elizabeth Armstrong and Laura Hamilton conducted pathways analyses to explore how students traversed (or attempted to traverse) higher education.[8] Specifically, they documented students' attempts to navigate pathways focused on (a) partying and socializing, (b) professional and career development, and (c) upward mobility. Less socioeconomically advantaged women at the university often struggled to find their way if they engaged with the "party pathway," especially if they took part in the Greek social system seemingly designed for their more advantaged peers who could participate in the "party pathway" with little impact on their future prospects. Students who engaged in the "mobility pathway" or "professional pathway" focused more on academics, but students from lower-income families often did not have the parental resources (fiscal and otherwise) to secure these professional opportunities.

In articulating their contributions, Armstrong and Hamilton describe sociological perspectives on how these pathways take shape, noting that, when an institution "structures the interests of a constituency into its organizational edifice, we say that it has created a 'pathway.'"[9] Their work underscored the fact that the journeys students take through higher education are not simply about student choices. Rather, colleges and universities play a crucial role in shaping these journeys by determining which resources, opportunities, constraints, and other normative institutional arrangements are present.

While qualitative scholars have been pushing forward the pathways metaphor, recent quantitative and mixed-methods research has illuminated fine-grained variation in these routes through college. For instance, Sorathan Chaturapruek and colleagues relied on "digital trace data" from logged clicks on a course exploration website paired with qualitative interviews to examine how students made course-selection decisions. Even with over 700 courses functionally available to students, they found that, on average, by the time students were exploring online, they considered only a small number (nine) of courses in their first academic term, and that the options they considered were predictive of the major students declared 2 years later.[10] Understanding what happens in this selection process may be crucial to revealing how early decision-making impacts future outcomes.

As students settle into college life and decide how to spend their time, it is also critical to understand the role extracurriculars play in undergraduate pathways. Research has shown students dedicate equal or less time to their studies as compared to extracurricular activities, which provide students with community, friendships, resources, and a sense of belonging on campus. An intersectional lens helps to uncover the ways students navigate pathways to becoming involved on campus. Where prior research focused primarily on quantitative assessments of participation in extracurricular outlets, Blake Silver used interviews with 80 first-year students to examine how they approached, experienced, and managed involvement. Findings revealed that while social class inequality influenced how students found extracurricular activities, the intersections of race and gender informed experiences within those outlets. Women and students of color frequently had their sense of belonging disrupted by peer expectations for stereotypical self-presentation. White men, by contrast, often felt embraced by peers in ways that fostered a durable sense of belonging. These uneven experiences led some women and students of color to reconfigure their involvement, a process where additional socioeconomic inequality emerged.[11]

Related work is being done to understand how undergraduate pathways are connected to career pathways. Reporting on findings from longitudinal interviews with 91 college seniors, Corey Moss-Pech documented the enhanced value of internships that students secured through institutionalized paths such as on-campus career fairs. Participants who took part in these "career conveyor belt internships" tended to receive full-time employment offers from the same companies, while those who took part in non-institutionalized internships were rarely offered employment and hence took longer to find full-time jobs after graduation.[12]

The full complexities of students' pathways, shaped by the juncture of available opportunities and student decisions, is only beginning to be understood. Yet findings like these make clear that the study of undergraduate pathways and subsequent interventions hold great possibility. As scholars note, work in this area has the potential to combat inequality in student experiences, degree completion, and career opportunities. It is this potential that we explore next in our recommendations and solutions.

Recommendations and solutions

The recent advances in the study of inequality in college student experiences summarized previously have unearthed promising avenues for combatting inequality and fostering success for broader populations of students. Some of these avenues point to ways to better understand students' journeys through higher education with empirical research as a first step toward improving higher education. Other avenues build from what we already know to direct immediate improvements to postsecondary institutions and the higher education landscape more broadly. We recommend several strategies to inform research, policy, and practice in postsecondary education.

Expanding undergraduate educational pathways research

- Scholars have begun advocating for understanding students' journeys through higher education using a pathways-based approach, a more nuanced way to think about college journeys that includes longitudinal understanding of sequences of progress and iterative decision-making.[13] We agree and advocate for research that addresses students' broader experiences as they navigate colleges and universities, including their extracurricular involvement.
- In the new world of big data and burgeoning computational methods (natural language processing, network analysis, and so on) more

questions can be asked and answered in the education space. Datasets comprised of course enrollment information, transcripts, syllabi, and even individual assignments are allowing more nuanced quantitative analysis of undergraduate pathways and sequential processes. Involvement transcripts, student résumés, graduate school applications, and other documentation of extracurricular participation could offer comparable insights about experiences in the extracurricular realm.

- Alongside these methods, it is also important to use longitudinal interview-based, ethnographic, and other qualitative approaches to explore students' educational journeys and take into account students' voices, narratives, and perspectives when trying to understand their decision-making and college experiences.
- Sociologists should specify how institutional contexts and normative institutional arrangements shape the availability of college pathways across a range of educational settings—with a focus on the institutions that house the most students in postsecondary education (community colleges and public, 4-year colleges and universities).
- Life course research suggests that for many middle- and upper-class families, college is seen as an important component of emerging adulthood, a steppingstone in human development. It is important to parse these experiences from those whose main objective in higher education is economic mobility and degree completion, examining students' broader objectives and narratives about their higher education experiences.
- As this research develops, dynamic intersectional approaches should be leveraged. As students move through various forms of involvement, different intersectional identities may become more or less salient and influential. Research that is only attentive to one or two dimensions of lived experience at a time may miss the complexity of how students navigate their ways to, through, and beyond various opportunities.
- Additionally, scholars will need to pay attention not only to the paths students take, but also to those they considered. The opportunities students contemplate and the approaches they use to make decisions can have consequences for students above and beyond the eventual routes they select.[14]
- All of this work should benefit from the strengths that make pathways research especially effective, namely attention to the sequencing, processes, and cumulative impacts of how students navigate college opportunities. Research should attend to specific stages of degree progress (first year, transfer, last year, and so on), which is necessary to understand the longitudinal nature of college experiences and corresponding choices, priorities, capital development, and impact.
- We encourage researchers to focus on the role of the university in shaping undergraduate pathways; institutions determine the general education

requirements, the courses and majors offered, financial aid packages, extracurricular funding, and residence hall assignments—all of which substantially impact the undergraduate experience.

Championing pathways-informed policy and practice

- Attention to undergraduate educational pathways can inform the ways faculty, administrators, and other higher education leaders shape policy and practice in a variety of institutions.[15] While the contours of university bureaucracy can sometimes obstruct efforts to understand and support students in a holistic manner, a focus on pathways can help to center student perspectives and experiences.
- If undergraduate success requires preexisting familiarity with college, parental involvement, or family connections for success, rather than institutional resources and support, colleges and universities are at risk of perpetuating inequality. Institutions must ensure that the pathways they build are complete with the tools students need to succeed. Administrators and policy makers who value college affordability, equal opportunity, and degree completion must ensure that pathways through college are clear and easily navigable.
- Universities need to structure educational pathways in ways that make requirements straightforward without penalizing students who need to explore their options or change course. Such priorities can be difficult to balance but are made easier with attention to the specific sequencing of educational opportunities. Research on path dependencies in undergraduate academic progress can illuminate the challenges and opportunities involved in this work.
- Higher education leaders should coordinate across units and divisions to support students' journeys through higher education. This will involve connecting student affairs and academic affairs professionals in the shared work of understanding and supporting students' broader patterns of navigating engagement within and beyond the classroom.
- Higher education professionals should be wary of the widespread promotion of "follow your passion" guidance, which has been shown to perpetuate inequality based on social class, race, and gender.[16] Students should have ample opportunities to explore their options, but such exploration should not require that they sacrifice their academic progress or mobility projects.
- Similarly, higher education leaders must ensure that the pathways available to students align with their institutions' priorities and values. When party pathways are easier to find than mobility pathways, for example, institutions are failing to uphold the aims articulated in their mission statements.

- We urge careful attention be paid to introductory courses in a range of fields of study, as early experiences (both academically and socially) can have a large impact on the fields students will consider—this is especially true of STEM courses.
- Early opportunities for involvement beyond the classroom, which students may encounter through orientations, first-week programming, and other first-year experiences, should be strategically promoted to allow accessible points of entry to the students who could benefit most from high-impact learning, professional development, and organizations that foster inclusion and belonging.
- Faculty, staff, and administrators should enlist the support of data and assessment professionals in designing systems that can help identify students who could benefit from specific resources, interventions, and opportunities at specific moments in their educational journeys.
- As we learn more about the unique pathways students use to navigate curricular and extracurricular engagement, practitioners and policy makers should strategize about how to weave both opportunities and resources into various pathways. When resources and opportunities are offered only on a self-serve basis, students who would most benefit from them are often the last to gain access.

Notes

[1] Kizilcec et al (2023).
[2] Arum et al (2018).
[3] Stevens, M. L., Armstrong, E. A., and Arum, R. (2008) Sieve, incubator, temple, hub: empirical and theoretical advances in the sociology of higher education. *Annual Review of Sociology*, 34(1): 127–51.
[4] Harrison et al (2022).
[5] Shandra (2022).
[6] Collins and Bilge (2020).
[7] Haynes, C., Joseph, N. M., Patton, L. D., Stewart, S., and Allen, E. L. (2020) Toward an understanding of intersectionality methodology: a 30-year literature synthesis of Black women's experiences in higher education. *Review of Educational Research*, 90(6): 751–87.
[8] Armstrong and Hamilton (2013).
[9] Armstrong and Hamilton (2013, p 15).
[10] Chaturapruek et al (2021).
[11] Silver (2020).
[12] Moss-Pech (2021).
[13] The authors would like to thank the researchers and practitioners who are part of the Pathways Network for providing a forum for exploring and sharing pathways research (https://pathways.stanford.edu/).
[14] Chaturapruek et al (2021).
[15] Blake Silver would like to acknowledge the support of the faculty and staff of George Mason University's Honors College, who have been part of numerous conversations about creating pathways-informed policies and practices.
[16] Cech (2021).

Key resources

Armstrong, E. A. and Hamilton, L. T. (2013) *Paying For the Party: How College Maintains Inequality*. Harvard University Press.

Arum, R., Roksa, J., Cruz, J., and Silver, B. (2018) Student experiences in college, in B. Schneider (Ed), *Handbook of the Sociology of Education in the 21st Century*. Springer, 385–403.

Cech, E. A. (2021) *The Trouble with Passion: How Searching for Fulfillment at Work Fosters Inequality*. University of California Press.

Chaturapruek, S., Dalberg, T., Thompson, M. E., Giebel, S., Harrison, M. H., Johari et al (2021) Studying undergraduate course consideration at scale. *AERA open*, 7, https://doi.org/10.1177/2332858421991148.

Collins, P. H. and Bilge, S. (2020) *Intersectionality*. John Wiley & Sons.

Harrison, M. H., Hernandez, P. A., and Stevens, M. L. (2022) Should I start at math 101? Content repetition as an academic strategy in elective curriculums. *Sociology of Education*, 95(2): 133–52.

Kizilcec, R. F., Baker, R. B., Bruch, E., Cortes, K. E., Hamilton, L. T., Lang, D. N. et al (2023) From pipelines to pathways in the study of academic progress. *Science*, 380(6643): 344–7.

Moss-Pech, C. (2021) The career conveyor belt: how internships lead to unequal labor market outcomes among college graduates. *Qualitative Sociology*, 44: 77–102.

Shandra, C. L. (2022). Internship participation in the United States by student and school characteristics, 1994 to 2017. *Socius*, 8, https://doi.org/10.1177/23780231221121058.

Silver, B. R. (2020). Inequality in the extracurriculum: how class, race, and gender shape college involvement. *Sociological Forum*, 35(4): 1290–314.

PART III

Food insecurity

EIGHT

Addressing food insecurity through community-informed food retailer implementation

Drew Bonner and Katie Kerstetter

The problem

Food access and food insecurity are topics of great consequence within public health, city planning, and public policy conversations. Food insecurity is a "lack of consistent access to enough food for every person in a household to live an active, healthy life."[1]

While food access conversations have rightfully interrogated institutional policies and practices, the central stakeholders—the community and citizens experiencing limited food access—have been mainly silenced from these conversations. This chapter will analyze the problem of current governmental policies and commercial agricultural practices, outlining the resulting issues of food insecurity perpetuated when community collaboration and citizen participation disappear from the agricultural production and distribution processes. We argue that food retailers are oriented towards generating profits, promoting the commodification of food, and perpetuating systemic health and social inequities through the disparate implementation of food retailer locations. We also argue that discriminatory zoning and land-use practices have facilitated diminished power and decision-making abilities for community residents in food production and distribution. Subsequently, these communities experience increased issues related to food insecurity, which may be more equitably addressed within a more participatory and community-based food system. We advocate for the necessity of community-informed food distribution and grocery stores and call for collaboration between city officials, urban planning professionals, and community residents to implement community-informed and culturally responsive food retailers and agricultural structures.

Since the 1970s, national agricultural policies have spurred an increase in the mass production of food and commodity crops alongside the changing landscape of food retail outlets.[2] Historical land restrictions and zoning policies have stifled local and community-based agricultural production by reserving agricultural land for profit-oriented corporations and factory farms and creating land acquisition and capacity-building barriers for local and community-based initiatives.[3] Grocery stores have become a part of the corporate system, with the focus now more on profit and efficiency. At the same time, the importance of societal health and equity remains an afterthought in implementing food retailer locations.[4]

Governmental food system policies and practices have perpetuated food commodification and insecurity, creating a need for equity-based food supply-chain implementation and support for subsistence, cooperative, and urban farming practices.[5] Consequently, the communities purchasing and consuming foods from these commercial retailers have disappeared from the agricultural production and distribution processes, perpetuating food insecurity issues.[6] Historically, food insecurity has intertwined with systemic racism, as historical economic marginalization from employment and generational wealth, as well as restrictions from land ownership, has created areas of decreased availability of food in communities of color through a process readily identified as food apartheid.[7]

Research evidence

The commercialization of food influences retailers to engage in strategies that maximize profits, facilitating disparities in the spatial distribution of food retailers and disparities in the concentration of nutrient-dense foods within those retailers.[8] The disparate development of grocery retailer locations is perpetuated through zoning policies and food system planning practices that are not equity-based or community-informed.[9] Commercial food retailers often operate in locations that maximize profits, perpetuating socioeconomic marginalization issues for disadvantaged communities. For example, in Washington, D.C., food retailers' density and spatial distribution are consistent with socioeconomic status boundaries, with most commercial grocery stores and food retailers located within higher-income areas.[10] Consequently, neighborhoods of lower socioeconomic status have fewer grocery stores and must travel greater distances to food retailers, challenging food access.[11]

Institutionalized racism is also perpetuated within the food system, as communities of color are most often negatively impacted by disparate food retailer implementation practices due to over-representation in lower socioeconomic status areas.[12] Food apartheid has facilitated increased food insecurity and nutritional deficiencies within communities of color by promoting economic marginalization, restrictions on land ownership, and diminished concentrations of nutrient-dense foods and food retailers.[13] The limited number of food retailers in socioeconomically disadvantaged and racially marginalized communities perpetuates an economic burden of increased costs related to accessing and purchasing produce as companies and corporations seek to maximize profits through the limited supply and demand of groceries in food-insecure areas.[14]

Scholars have widely demonstrated that socioeconomically marginalized communities often have the knowledge and resources necessary for maintenance and efficacy. However, they are regularly prevented from enacting community developmental power due to bureaucratic, political, and punitive governmental policies.[15] Conversely, these communities regularly enact power by organizing outside the political and economic system.

For example, Ashanti Reese demonstrated that Black community members in Washington D.C. responded to the disparate food insecurity issues by creating "geographies of self-reliance," in which community innovations of resource sharing, gleaning, and local agricultural practices fortified food access in areas experiencing food apartheid.[16] Similarly, Joshua Sbicca analyzed how community aid was developed in predominantly Black residential areas of Oakland, California, by engaging formerly incarcerated members of the Black community to support and lead the efforts of urban farming and food distribution.[17] These community efforts increased food security and provided economic opportunities for the formerly incarcerated community members, creating a two-fold effect of restorative justice by diminishing the effects of historical lineages of food apartheid and mass incarceration.

Community innovations such as these demonstrate the innovative power of communities to organize their food systems in historically marginalized areas.[18] However, more than communities' innovative power is needed adequately to address the issue of food insecurity. Communities must be formally and equitably included in governmental food systems policy decisions, collaboratively engaging with governmental officials to develop strategies that increase access to food retailers and resources for communities to build their food systems.

Recommendations and solutions

Food insecurity and disparate food retailer implementation require national policies supporting community-informed grocery outlet implementation and community-based agricultural production and distribution. Equity-based policies must collaboratively emerge utilizing multi-level partnerships between federal organizations, city officials, food systems planners, community organizations, and community members to ensure that all relevant stakeholders contribute to each level of the agricultural and production process. In the following paragraphs, we outline proposed strategies that federal organizations, city officials, and food systems planning professionals may utilize to enact equity-based processes to improve community participation in food retailer implementation strategies.

- National support for community-based food retailers

  To support the increased availability of nutrient-dense food items in food-insecure communities, we recommend implementing federal funding to establish community-based food retailers in communities without access to food retailers. These community-based food retailers would serve as "healthy food hubs," offering a sufficient quantity of nutrient-dense food items proportionate to the needs of each community. The adequate amount of nutrient-dense food would be collaboratively established by community-based partners and federal offices, such as USDA, to ensure that food items within these food retailers are culturally relevant and of sufficient quality. Funding would be provided through a federal grant or demonstration program focused on serving communities with the lowest concentrations of food retailers. Guidelines about which communities would be eligible for these programs should be community-informed, along with the type of community participation required. Implementing this program involves the creation of Community Action Networks in each food hub area to inform the development of each food retailer.

- National support for community-based and subsistence farming practices

  To support the increased availability of nutrient-dense foods in food-insecure communities, we recommend implementing governmental support for micro-farming, subsistence farming, and cooperative farming practices. Governmental support could appear in financial resources, farming materials, and logistical support for agricultural production and distribution at the community level. Federal and local government offices could develop community partnerships with community gardens and school gardens, support direct farming activities by small, community-based farmers, and increase distribution opportunities for local cooperative farming. The support may include financial assistance with securing land and materials to begin farming activities, ensuring resources are available to these community-level and cooperative farms, and providing technical assistance and training for establishing supply-chain and distribution outlets to get the food items produced into grocery stores and community-based food retailers.

- National support for farmers and community-based food retailers from historically underserved communities

  To adequately address food apartheid and support national equity-based initiatives to increase food access in underserved communities, we recommend increased federal funding and support for BIPOC farmers within the food system. National funding should be provided to support farmers and agricultural producers in underserved communities, particularly Black farmers, which will assist them with equitably addressing implementation and maintenance costs associated with agriculture, farming, and distribution. National support should be available to

BIPOC farmers to assist in the technical application of agricultural activities, including support from offices such as USDA, to assist with producing, marketing, and selling food items in underserved populations and communities experiencing food insecurity.

- Partnerships between local government planners, commercial food retailers, and community-based organizations for community-informed food retailer implementation

  To establish an equity-based approach to commercial food retailer implementation, we recommend national policy to incentivize community-informed implementation of food retailer spaces within communities, both urban and rural. Community members and community-led organizations would be directly involved in selecting and implementing food retailer locations. The collaboration between local planners, commercial food retailers, and community members will facilitate an equitable approach to grocery store implementation, increasing the likelihood that food retailers may be physically accessible to a more equitable population distribution.[19] The community-informed implementation of local food systems planning will also ensure that the availability of food items at these retailer locations will be culturally relevant and culturally responsive to the respective communities that host the food retailers. National policies to incentivize these partnerships may include funding to revise zoning and other policies, formal partnerships with community-based organizations, and establishing community networks in each city to ensure that community members adequately contribute to food systems planning activities.

- Establishing national networks between grocery retailers and community-aid organizations

  To support the increased density of food retailers within communities experiencing food insecurity, we recommend the development of national networks and partnerships between grocery outlets and mutual aid groups, farmers markets, and other community-developed alternative food networks. The networks and partnerships would promote an equity-based distribution initiative that connects grocery outlets with alternative food hubs so that they may receive nutrient-dense food items to serve to the community at little to no cost. While we acknowledge the complex history of alternative food networks and the challenges and denigrations of food banks providing communities with foods that are deemed undesirable, we believe that connections between commercial food retailers and these alternative food networks may mitigate the issue of food insecurity and increase the potential consumption of foods before expiration, establishing greater connection and collaboration.[20] The networks and partnerships between grocery outlets and mutual aid groups, farmers markets, and other community-developed alternative food networks will assist in the process of incorporating nutrient-dense and viable (non-expired) foods at these alternative food outlets, while also combating issues of food waste within the grocery outlet supply-chain.[21]

• National support for gleaning programs and gift economy networks

To further support food access and affordability of food items, we recommend increased national recognition and funding of community-developed food networks and gift economies, such as mutual aid groups and food banks. These food hubs often serve as primary retail networks in the spatially incongruent grocery outlets and food retailers system. This dynamic is particularly true for individuals within underserved and socioeconomically disadvantaged communities, as individuals may supplement their income by securing food from food banks and mutual aid groups. A national policy would mandate support for these alternative food networks through grants and subsidies to increase the capacity and quantity of nutrient-dense foods available at these outlets.

• National support for affordable nutrient-dense foods

An essential part of increasing equitable access to food is ensuring that nutrient-dense foods are affordable to all households. We commend the USDA for revising the Supplemental Nutrition Assistance Program's (SNAP) Thrifty Food Plan to reflect current food prices and dietary recommendations better. However, even with these changes and annual inflation adjustments, SNAP benefits still do not fully cover the cost of a modest meal in 78 percent of counties in the US.[22] We recommend increasing funding for SNAP benefits to adequately cover the cost of preparing and consuming nutrient-dense foods for all households.

Our analysis of the national food system has provided evidence for community informed food retailer implementation. We argue that national agricultural policies and commercial food retailer practices have promoted the commodification of the food system, and the disparate implementation of food retailer locations, consequently perpetuating systemic health and social inequities. We also argue that discriminatory zoning and land-use practices have facilitated diminished power and decision-making abilities for community residents in food production and distribution. Subsequently, these communities experience increased issues related to food insecurity, which may be more equitably addressed within a more participatory and community-based food system. Thus, we continue to advocate for the formal implementation of community-informed food distribution strategies, outlining recommendations for national equity-based policies that promote community participation in food retailer implementation strategies and community-based agricultural production and distribution. We advocate for establishing collaborative multi-level partnerships between governmental stakeholders, urban planning professionals, community-based organizations, and community residents to implement culturally responsive agricultural structures. We hope these recommendations motivate social action and public policy for the advancement of a more equitable food system.

Notes

[1] Feeding America (2023) What is food insecurity? Available from: https://www.feeding america.org/hunger-in-america/food-insecurity#:~:text=The%20USDA%20defines%20f ood%20insecurity

[2] Flesher, J. (2020) Factory farms provide abundant food, but environment suffers. PBS NewsHour, [online] February 6. Available from: https://www.pbs.org/newshour/econ omy/factory-farms-provide-abundant-food-but-environment-suffers; Healthy Food Policy Project (2020) Zoning for urban agriculture: a guide for updating your city's laws to support healthy food production and access. Available from: https://healthyfoodpo licyproject.org/key-issues/zoning-for-urban-agriculture; Lakhani, N., Uteuova, A., and Chang, A. (2021) Revealed: the true extent of America's food monopolies, and who pays the price. *The Guardian*, [online], July 14. Available from: https://www.theguardian.com/ environment/ng-interactive/2021/jul/14/food-monopoly-meals-profits-data-investigat ion; McGreal, C. (2019) How America's food giants swallowed the family farms. *The Guardian* [online], March 10. Available from: https://www.theguardian.com/environm ent/2019/mar/09/american-food-giants-swallow-the-family-farms-iowa.

[3] Flesher (2020), see note 3; Healthy Food Policy Project (2020), see note 3; McGreal (2019), see note 3; United States Environmental Protect Agency (2018) Laws and regulations that apply to your agricultural operation by farm activity. Available from: https://www. epa.gov/agriculture/laws-and-regulations-apply-your-agricultural-operation-farm-activ ity; U.S. Department of the Interior Bureau of Land Management (2021) More than survival, the subsistence tradition sustains meaning for rural Alaska natives and non-native residents alike. Bureau of Land Management. Available from: https://www.blm.gov/ blog/2021-08-17/more-survival-subsistence-tradition-sustains-meaning-rural-alaska-nati ves-and-non.

[4] Cronin, D. (2023) Food prices are still high. What role do record corporate profits play in food inflation? Civil Eats. Available from: https://civileats.com/2023/05/22/food-pri ces-are-still-high-what-role-do-corporate-profits-play/; Schweizer, E. (2022) How profit inflation made your groceries so damn expensive. *Forbes*. Available from: https://www. forbes.com/sites/errolschweizer/2022/09/12/how-profit-inflation-made-your-grocer ies-so-damn-expensive/?sh=5c1695242eb9

[5] Flesher (2020), see note 3; Haines (2018); Healthy Food Policy Project (2020) see note 3; Lakhani et al (2021), see note 3; McGreal (2019), see note 3; Raja et al (2014) Rustbelt radicalism: a decade of food systems planning practice in Buffalo, New York (US). *Journal of Agriculture, Food Systems, and Community Development*, 4(4): 173–89; Shirvell, B. (2023) For urban farmers, community organizing can be key to easing zoning constraints. Modern Farmer. Available from: https://modernfarmer.com/2023/05/for-urban-farm ers-community-organizing-can-be-key-to-easing-zoning-constraints/; U.S. Department of the Interior Bureau of Land Management (2021), see note 4.

[6] Cronin (2023), see note 5; Crowe et al (2018) Barriers to food security and community stress in an urban food desert. *Urban Science*, 2(2): 46. Kim (2023); Raja et al (2014), see note 6; Schweizer (2022), see note 5; Shirvell (2023), see note 6.

[7] Brones, A. (2018) Karen Washington: it's not a food desert, it's food apartheid. *Guernica* [online], May 7. Available from: https://www.guernicamag.com/karen-washington-its-not-a-food-desert-its-food-apartheid/; Burrell, D. N. (2022) Food apartheid and food insecurity. *International Journal of Public and Private Perspectives on Healthcare, Culture, and the Environment*, 6(1): 1–11; Reese (2019); Rowlands, D., Donoghoe, M., and Perry,

A. M. (2023) What the lack of premium grocery stores says about disinvestment in Black neighborhoods. Brookings. Available from: https://www.brookings.edu/articles/what-the-lack-of-premium-grocery-stores-says-about-disinvestment-in-black-neighborhoods/; Sevilla, N. (2021) *Food Apartheid: Racialized Access to Healthy Affordable Food*. NRDC [online], April 2. Available from: https://www.nrdc.org/bio/nina-sevilla/food-aparth eid-racialized-access-healthy-affordable-food.

[8] Logan, T. M., Anderson, M. J., Williams, T. G., and Conrow, L. (2021) Measuring inequalities in urban systems: an approach for evaluating the distribution of amenities and burdens. *Computers, Environment and Urban Systems*, 86: 101590; Pinstrup-Andersen, P. (2009) Food security: definition and measurement. *Food Security*, 1(1): 5–7: Ver Ploeg, M., Dutko, P., and Breneman, V. (2014) Measuring food access and food deserts for policy purposes. *Applied Economic Perspectives and Policy*, 37(2): 205–25.

[9] Haines (2018); Slade et al, T. (2016) Urban planning roles in responding to food security needs. *Journal of Agriculture, Food Systems, and Community Development*, 7(1): 33–48.

[10] D.C. Food Policy Council (2014) 2018 grocery stores. Available from: https://www.arcgis.com/home/webmap/viewer.html?webmap=0713e9658f5f48559a77101cf2575 d74&extent=-77.2998,38.7054,-76.6217,39.0312.

[11] Baskin, M. (2023) More than one-third of D.C. residents face food insecurity, report shows. DCist. Available from: https://dcist.com/story/23/09/12/dc-food-insecurity-rep ort/; D.C. Food Policy Council (2014), see note 11.

[12] Odoms-Young, A., and Bruce, M. A. (2018) Examining the impact of structural racism on food insecurity. *Family & Community Health*, 41(2), S3–6; Ramírez, M. M. (2014) The elusive inclusive: Black food geographies and racialized food spaces. *Antipode*, 47(3): 748–69. Reese (2019).

[13] Brones (2018), see note 8; Burrell (2022), see note 8; Reese (2019); Rowlands et al (2023), see note 8; Sevilla (2021).

[14] Ivanova, I. (2023) Food prices are rising at the highest rate in decades. Here's where that money goes. CBS News [online] April 7. Available from: https://www.cbsnews.com/news/food-prices-inflation-inputs-profits-heres-where-that-money-goes/; Schwartz, N. D. and Marcos, C. M. (2021) Higher food prices hit the poor and those who help them. *The New York Times* [online], October 27. Available from: https://www.nytimes.com/2021/10/27/business/economy/food-prices-us.html; Wiener-Bronner, D. (2023) The cost of food is down, but grocery bills are still up. Here's why. CNN [online], March 8. Available from: https://www.cnn.com/2023/03/08/economy/food-prices-inflation/index.html.

[15] Kaur, R., Winkler, M., John, S., DeAngelo, J., Dombrowski, R., Hickson, A. et al (2022) Forms of community engagement in neighborhood food retail: healthy community stores case study project. *International Journal of Environmental Research and Public Health*, 19(12): 6986; Raja et al (2014), see note 6; Reese (2019); Sbicca, J. (2016) These bars can't hold us back: plowing incarcerated geographies with restorative food justice. *Antipode*, 48(5): 1359–79; Slade et al (2016), see note 10.

[16] Reese (2019).

[17] Sbicca (2016), see note 16.

[18] Raja et al (2014), see note 6; Reese (2019); Sbicca (2016), see note 16.

[19] Bublitz, M. G., Peracchio, L. A., Dadzie, C. A., Escalas, J. E., Hansen, J., Hutton, M. et al (2019) Food access for all: empowering innovative local infrastructure. *Journal of Business Research*, 100: 354–65; Lee, C., Bassam, E. R. W., and Kuhn, I. (2021) Community-oriented actions by food retailers to support community well-being: a systematic scoping review. *Public Health*, 201: 115–24; Liao, L., Warner, M. E., and Homsy, G. C. (2019) Sustainability's forgotten third E: what influences local government actions on social equity? *Local Environment*, 24(12): 1197–208.

[20] McMillan, T. (2014) The new face of hunger. *National Geographic*. Available from: https://www.nationalgeographic.com/foodfeatures/hunger/. Poppendieck, J. (1999) *Sweet Charity? Emergency Food and the End of Entitlement*. Penguin; Vitiello, D., Grisso, J. A., Whiteside, K. L., and Fischman, R. (2015) From commodity surplus to food justice: food banks and local agriculture in the United States. *Agriculture and Human Values*, 32(3): 419–30.

[21] Lofton, S., Kersten, M., Simonovich, S. D., and Martin, A. (2021) Highlighting the role of mutual aid in Chicago during COVID-19: could mutual aid be the solution to food insecurity in underserved urban communities? *Public Health Nutrition*, 25(1): 1–10. Ramjug, P. (2022). *Supermarkets help their bottom line when they donate to food banks*. Northeastern Global News [online], February 22. Available from: https://news.northeastern.edu/2022/02/22/food-supply-chain/; Roman-Alcalá, A. (2020); Unite US (2023) How food banks can expand their reach and impact. UniteUS.com. Available from: https://uniteus.com/blog/food-banks-and-cross-sector-collaboration/; United States Environmental Protect Agency (2018), see note 4.

[22] Urban Institute (2023).

Key resources

Bublitz, M. G., Peracchio, L. A., Dadzie, C. A., Escalas, J. E., Hansen, J., Hutton, M. et al (2019) Food access for all: empowering innovative local infrastructure. *Journal of Business Research*, 100: 354–65.

Chrisinger, B. W. (2022) Getting to root causes: why equity must be at the center of planning and public health collaboration. *Journal of the American Planning Association*, 89(2): 160–6.

Cronin, D. (2023) What role do record corporate profits play in food inflation? Civil Eats. Available from: https://civileats.com/2023/05/22/food-prices-are-still-high-what-role-do-corporate-profits-play/

Haines, A. (2018) What does zoning have to do with local food systems? *Journal of Agriculture, Food Systems, and Community Development*, 8(B): 175–90.

Kim, W. (2023) Prices at the supermarket keep rising. So do corporate profits. *Vox* [online] March 17. Available from: https://www.vox.com/money/23641875/food-grocery-inflation-prices-billionaires

Lee, C., Bassam, E. R. W. and Kuhn, I. (2021) Community-oriented actions by food retailers to support community well-being: a systematic scoping review. *Public Health*, 201: 115–124.

Reese, A. M. (2019) *Black Food Geographies: Race, Self-Reliance, and Food Access in* Washington, D.C.: University of North Carolina Press.

Roman-Alcalá, A. (2020) Op-ed: we can build a better food system through mutual aid. Civil Eats. Available from: https://civileats.com/2020/06/26/op-ed-we-can-build-a-better-food-system-through-mutual-aid/

Sevilla, N. (2021) Food apartheid: racialized access to healthy affordable food. NRDC. Available from: https://www.nrdc.org/bio/nina-sevilla/food-apartheid-racialized-access-healthy-affordable-food

Urban Institute (2023) Does SNAP cover the cost of a meal in your county? Urban Institute. Available from: https://www.urban.org/data-tools/does-snap-cover-cost-meal-your-county-2022

How inflation and food deserts made a bad poverty measure worse—and what we can do about it

Teresa A. Sullivan

The problem

Even after substantial post–COVID economic recovery, 38 million individual Americans (11.6 percent) live in poverty according to the federal measuring-stick, known as the Federal Poverty Level (FPL). This measuring-stick overlooks key aspects of food insecurity but is nevertheless consequential in determining how poverty funds are distributed.

Food is the most basic need for families. The origin of the FPL, described in this chapter, recognized this fact. But the FPL incorporated two flawed assumptions. The first assumption was that food prices would inflate at the same rate as all other goods and services. The second assumption was that poor people would spend a constant fraction of their income on food, paying the same prices for food as better-off Americans do. In fact, food prices have recently inflated faster than other goods, and people in poverty are likely to have more trouble finding food and to pay higher prices for the food they find.

The FPL affects families' eligibility for social safety net programs. All federal agencies are expected to use the FPL or a modification of FPL to qualify individuals and families to receive Medicaid, free school lunches, Head Start, and other safety-net programs.

Entire communities qualify for federal poverty funding based on the proportion of their residents earning less than the FPL. Persistent poverty counties have smaller populations and higher proportions of under-represented minorities, and they are more likely to be rural. The 409 persistent-poverty counties, so designated by the application of the FPL, are eligible to receive billions of dollars from 247 different federal programs. These programs support local infrastructure such as public works and technology upgrades. The flaws in the FPL make it likely that additional counties might qualify under a revised measure. By underestimating poverty, the FPL results in inadequate funds that are inequitably distributed among communities.

Potential solutions include strong leadership from the White House, cooperation among a dozen federal agencies, changes in federal law, action by state and local leaders, and voter vigilance. This chapter outlines the origin of the problem and the steps that will improve it.

Research evidence

Few statistical measures have received the intense, continuous research scrutiny that poverty measures have received. The appropriate federal role in alleviating poverty has been vigorously debated for decades. The Great Depression of the 1930s, when unemployment might have affected over a third of the population, persuaded many people that systemic economic dislocation caused poverty, and not just individuals' misfortunes or behavior. Beginning with the New Deal of the Franklin D. Roosevelt administration (1933–45), the federal government assumed a role in alleviating poverty because only the government was perceived as large enough to effect change.

When President Lyndon B. Johnson's administration declared a *War on Poverty*, the government needed to measure poverty. It was practically and politically desirable to develop an objective, quantitative measure that could be analyzed and remeasured periodically. The federal poverty level has existed, with minor tweaks, since the mid-1960s. The FPL prices the cost of a minimally adequate emergency diet and multiplies that number by three, an approach derived from research conducted between 1955 and 1960. The FPL is adjusted for family size and updated annually by the Consumer Price Index for Urban Consumers.[1] The food cost part of the FPL comes from a 1955 study in which the U.S. Department of Agriculture (USDA) developed four income-based food plans. The cheapest "economy" food plan was "designed for temporary or emergency use when funds are low."[2] Despite the designation of this minimal diet for temporary or emergency use, its cost became the basis for the poverty level.

In 1965, Mollie Orshansky, an economist with the Social Security Administration, determined from Department of Agriculture data that families of three or more persons spent about one third of their after-tax money income on food in 1955. Accordingly, she calculated poverty thresholds for families of three or more persons by taking the dollar costs of the economy food plan for families of those sizes and multiplying the costs by a factor of three. This was the first FPL.

A common misperception is that the FPL is linked to the minimum wage. In 2023 the poverty level for a single individual was $14,580. Although Orshansky developed the FPL using after-tax income, it is currently calculated with pre-tax income, resulting in even less disposable income for the household. Assuming that a single individual's cash income was solely from wages and salaries (as is true of 80 percent of the population), the hourly wage for a full-time, full-year worker with this level of earnings would average $6.80, well below the federal minimum wage of $7.75. By definition a single person working full-time and year-round (2000 hours) at the federal minimum age would earn $15,500 and cannot be poor. A couple who both worked full-time and year-round at minimum wage would earn $31,000, exceeding the 2023 FPL of $30,000 for a family of four, and so they and their two children would not be poor.[3]

- Inflation has invalidated the assumptions

    Orshansky proposed inflating the index by food price increases. In 1969, an interagency Poverty Level Review Committee decided to index the thresholds by the Consumer Price Index and not the per capita cost of the economy food plan. An implication of this decision is that food prices are assumed to inflate at the same rate as housing, transportation, clothing, and all the other things that households buy. This assumption is incorrect.

    Since the COVID pandemic, food has inflated at a faster rate than other purchases.[4] Between February 2022 and February 2023, the Consumer Price Index rose by 6 percent. But food prices were 9.5 percent higher in February 2023 than they had been 12 months earlier. Between 2020 and 2021 food prices rose by 11.4 percent. Relatively inexpensive foods consumed by low-income families had even higher inflation. Between 2020 and 2021, for example, the price of eggs rose 10.8 percent. Plain white bread showed steep increases that also varied by region, rising 27.4 percent in the Northeast and 17.8 percent in the Midwest.
- The 1:3 ratio may be outdated, especially depending on a household's location

    Setting aside whether a diet originally developed for emergency use is a humane baseline, the 1:3 ratio of food to other expenditures has fluctuated over time for the population in the lowest fifth of the income distribution. In 2021 the poorest families spent around 30 percent of their income on food. (By contrast, households in the highest income fifth spent only 7.6 percent of their income on food.)

    The ratio also fluctuates with geography.[5] People in poverty might end up spending larger proportions of their incomes on food because of their residence. In 2022 the USDA estimated that 53.6 million people lived in areas with low access to food.[6] Food deserts have limited food supplies and high food prices. Edible options in food deserts tend to be shelf-stable, high-sugar, high-fat processed foods instead of fresh food.

    Urban food deserts have few supermarkets and they are small with higher per-unit costs for each unit sold compared with suburban stores.

Inner-city supermarkets pass their higher costs to consumers. The cost of transporting food into crowded urban areas, for example, adds to the price mark-up. Without nearby inexpensive supermarkets, residents of low-income neighborhoods typically buy food at higher-priced convenience stores, fast food outlets, and mom–and–pop grocery stores. These small outlets typically charge prices that are 10 percent higher than supermarkets. Alternatively, low-income families can travel outside their neighborhood, but that trip adds the expense of transportation and time missed from work to the cost of food for the family.

The rural poor do not fare much better, because rural supermarket prices average about 4 percent more than urban supermarkets.

- The poverty level is unfairly administered

Federal agencies unfairly administer poverty funds. For example, Public Law 111-5 mandates the so-called 10-20-30 rule, which states that 10 percent of the funding for 247 federal programs must go to counties in which 20 percent of the population has been below the poverty level during 30 years of measurement. Currently 13 percent of all counties are designated persistent-poverty counties, 50 percent of which are rural. In 2021 the Government Accountability Office (the Congressional watchdog agency) issued a study showing that the federal agencies fall far below complying with the guideline, in effect cheating the poorest counties of funding.[7]

Recommendations and solutions

Just as poverty is a long-term problem, the efforts to alleviate poverty need long-term reevaluation. Addressing these issues will require coordination within both the executive and legislative branches of the federal government. State and local governments should also act.

- The Executive Branch should revise the current measure and propose the revision to Congress for adoption

The role of the White House is crucial in proposing a revised FPL measure to Congress for adoption because many federal agencies are involved in developing and using the FPL. The GAO has called for the Office of Management and Budget, located within the White House, to standardize the guidelines for distributing poverty funding.

How the data are collected illustrates the complexity of coordination among agencies. The underlying income data for the poverty level comes from the Current Population Survey, a monthly survey conducted by the Census Bureau, a part of the Department of Commerce, on behalf of the Bureau of Labor Statistics, which is also a part of the Department of Labor. The fraction of income spent on food comes from the Consumer

Expenditure Study, which the Census Bureau conducts annually for the Bureau of Labor Statistics.

The Departments of Treasury, Agriculture, Transportation, HHS, and Education, among others, use the FPL in their work. With so many players from the Executive Branch, it would take a large trans-agency task force to analyze and revise the current FPL. Such task forces have been deployed several times in the past, and it is time today to do it again. Computer resources unavailable in 1965 make more sophisticated adjustments possible today.

- Use the most recent food pricing data

  The USDA revised its 1955 study to develop a new diet called the "thrifty food plan." The language of "emergency use" has been dropped because the new plan incorporates attention to nutrition and cultural acceptability besides cost. Developed in 2018, the Thrifty Food Plan "represents a nutritious, practical, cost-effective diet prepared at home for a 'reference' family, which is defined in law as an adult male and female, ages 20–50, and two children, ages 6–8 and 9–11."[8] The USDA also reevaluated the cost of the plan, and in 2021 the revised cost became the basis for maximum SNAP benefit allocations. (SNAP, the Supplemental Nutritional Assistance Program, was formerly the Food Stamp program). These improvements, however, have not so far been incorporated into the FPL.

- Annually update what proportion of their income the poverty population spends on food

  The second step should be to examine Consumer Expenditure Studies for the expenditures of the lowest income quintile of families to derive the current proportion of their income spent on food. The ratio of food expenditures to total income should be evaluated periodically, preferably every year. The non-food portion of household expenditures can be annually inflated by the Consumer Price Index.

- Use the inflation factor for food to inflate the fraction of income spent on food

  The government calculates inflation of food, fuel, housing, and other expenditures separately, but the composite Consumer Price Index is used to inflate the poverty income level. One important step in a revision should be to price out the new thrifty food plan and then inflate that food portion of the FPL annually by rate of food inflation, not the overall inflation rate. The fraction of income that is not spent on food could then be inflated by the Consumer Price Index.

- Congress should clarify the pertinent laws

  Federal law defines the FPL, its measurement, and its annual adjustment by the Consumer Price Index (42 U.S.C. §9902(2)). This statute also provides for the Census Bureau to calculate the FPL. Congress should amend this law to mandate the above proposed changes.

Congress should also specify that all federal agencies use the revised FPL for all poverty-related actions. Besides the law defining the FPL, there is currently a patchwork of other poverty legislation. For example, different agencies use different datasets and methodologies to identify persistent-poverty counties for the 10-20-30 formula. The Economic Development Agency (EDA) used a methodology that identified one hundred more persistent-poverty counties than the other two agencies. Congress contributed to the confusion, because appropriations laws for 2017–20 required the agencies to use data from different years and sources, some of them outdated, to identify the counties. Besides the confusion, the varying approaches lead to underinvestment in poor counties.

Other laws and regulations require the use of percentages of the federal poverty threshold but give agencies leeway to set guidelines higher or lower than the FPL. This policy leads to inconsistency and confusion and Congress should reconsider these inconsistent uses. The IRS uses the FPL itself as a qualifier for items such as medical premium tax credits. Medicaid eligibility is based upon 138 percent of the FPL. This means that a family that is somewhat above the poverty level can still qualify for medical care. By contrast, the eligibility for other benefits from the Department of Health and Human Services have thresholds that are even lower than the poverty level. In 2017, for example, the FPL for a family of four was $25,283, but the HHS poverty guidelines to be "poor" were 2.3 percent **lower** at $24,600.

Congress should also recognize that agency funding mechanisms put persistent-poverty counties at a further disadvantage. Some federal funding programs are based upon successful submission of grant proposals. Many persistent-poverty counties lose funding because, ironically, they already have too little funding. As a result they lack experts to write successful grants, and they lack the local funding to match some grants (such as EPA's climate adaptation grants). Congress could alleviate these problems with a program to underwrite universities or state legislatures to provide grant-writers for persistent poverty counties. Congress could also provide grants-in-aid so that poverty counties could qualify for matching grants, or reduce the match required from a poverty area.

• State and local governments can address the issue of food deserts

Shrinking the food deserts or eliminating them altogether would help a family's food dollars stretch farther. If the available food is cheaper, or if transportation to get food requires less time and money, a family has more of its income available for other expenses. Tax incentives, for example, can encourage large supermarket chains to locate stores in food deserts. These incentives could take the form of relief from property or sales taxes for stores that locate within a food desert. Even public exhortation can be helpful. A city councilwoman in Austin, Texas, recently appealed to

HEB Stores, a large Texas grocery chain, to place a store in Del Valle, a low-income unincorporated community adjacent to Austin.

Local governments usually control public transit, directly or indirectly. Some cities' public transit provides a "museum bus" for tourists that makes a circuit of all the major museums. This idea could be adapted for a "food bus," ideally with no fare or a reduced fare, that makes a circuit of grocery stores, farmers markets, and food banks. The food bus should also have connectors to routes that serve low-income neighborhoods. Better transportation would allow low-income families to leave the food deserts to shop easily.

In general, improved public transportation could remove a major obstacle for families in poverty who need to access goods and services but cannot afford the expenses of a car, gasoline, licenses, and car maintenance.

As a short-run approach to alleviating food deserts, local governments can examine their zoning and other regulations that restrict where food trucks and mobile food banks may operate. Partnerships with farmers, such as Community Supported Agriculture, are programs that benefit both the farm family and the consumers by eliminating some of the middle actors; these programs often provide fresh food of higher quality and lower cost than that which is currently available. Through public schools and social services, families can be made aware of their eligibility for SNAP and other poverty relief programs.

- State governments could make localities more competitive for federal funding

  State governments can identify resources to help their persistent-poverty areas to compete for federal funds that are available only through grant applications. Besides persistent-poverty counties, there are housing authorities, school districts, sanitary districts, library districts, and transportation authorities that could be at a competitive disadvantage for federal funds.

- Voters can remember that poverty is still an issue in the United States

  Voters should hold public officials accountable for seeking solutions to food insecurity. Poverty is a struggle not only for millions of American families but also for hundreds of communities. Revising the FPL would provide both a sharper focus on the social problem and a better tool for alleviating it.

Notes

[1]   Orshansky, M. (1969) How poverty is measured. *Monthly Labor Review*, 92(2): 37–41.
[2]   Gordon, M. and Fisher, G. M. (1997) The Development and History of the U.S. Poverty Thresholds- A Brief Overview. GSS/SSS Newsletter [Newsletter of the Government Statistics Section and the Social Statistics Section of the American Statistical Association] https://aspe.hhs.gov/topics/poverty-economic-mobility/poverty-guidelines/further-resources-poverty-measurement-poverty-lines-their-history/history-poverty-thresho lds#:~:text=The%20poverty%20thresholds%20were%20originally,1965%20Social%20S ecurity%20Bulletin%20article

3   U.S. Department of Health and Human Services, Office of the Assistant Secretary for Planning and Evaluation, *Poverty Guidelines* (January 2023) https://aspe.hhs.gov/top ics/poverty-economic-mobility/poverty-guidelines. Alaska has a separate set of poverty levels because of its high cost of living but is the only geographic area with a separate poverty level.

4   U.S. Department of Agriculture, *Summary Findings: Food Price Outlook, 2023 and 2024* (November 2023). https://www.ers.usda.gov/data-products/food-price-outlook/summ ary-findings/

5   U.S. Department of Agriculture, Economic Research Service, *Food Access Research Atlas* (September 2023). https://www.ers.usda.gov/data-products/food-access-research-atlas.aspx

6   U.S. Department of Agriculture, *Economic Research Service, Food Access Research Atlas*

7   Elizabeth Kneebone, Tackling Persistent Poverty: Three Challenges for the 10-20-30 Plan (October 2016), Brookings Institution. https://www.brookings.edu/articles/tackling-per sistent-poverty-three-challenges-for-the-10-20-30-plan/; Government Accountability Office, Areas with High Poverty: Changing How the 10-20-30 Funding Formula is Applied Could Increase Impact in Persistent-Poverty Counties (2021). https://www.gao. gov/products/gao-21-470#:~:text=Some%20federal%20agencies%20have%20been,(per sistent%2Dpoverty%20counties)

8   U.S. Department of Agriculture, Food and Nutrition Service, *SNAP and the Thrifty Food Plan* (November 2023). https://www.fns.usda.gov/snap/thriftyfoodplan

Key resources

DeSilver, D. (2022) In the U.S. and around the world, inflation is high and getting higher. Pew Research Center. Available from: https://www.pewr esearch.org/short-reads/2022/06/15/in-the-u-s-and-around-the-world-inflation-is-high-and-getting-higher/

Desmond, M. (2023) *Poverty, by America.* Crown.

Fisher, G. M. (1997 [1992]) *The Development and History of the U.S. Poverty Thresholds: A Brief Overview.* U.S. Department of Health and Human Services. Available from: https://aspe.hhs.gov/topics/poverty-econo mic-mobility/poverty-guidelines/further-resources-poverty-measurem ent-poverty-lines-their-history/history-poverty thresholds#:~:text= The%20poverty%20thresholds%20were%20originally,1965%20Social%20 Security%20Bulletin%20article.

Government Accountability Office (2021) *Areas with High Poverty: Changing How the 10-20-30 Funding Formula Is Applied Could Increase Impact in Persistent-Poverty Counties* (GAO 21-470). Available from: https://www. gao.gov/assets/gao-21-470.pdf

Kaufman, P. R., MacDonald, J. M., Lutz, S. M., and Smallwood, D. M. (1997) *Do the Poor Pay More for Food? Item Selection and Price Differences Affect Low-Income Household Food Costs.* (Agricultural Economic Report 759). U.S. Department of Agriculture, Economic Research Service. Available from: https://naldc.nal.usda.gov/download/34238/PDF#:~:text=Groc ery%20stores%20in%20central%20cities,higher%20costs%20per%20u nit%20sold

National Academies of Sciences, Engineering, and Medicine (2023) *An Updated Measure of Poverty: (Re)Drawing the Line.* The National Academies Press.

Orshansky, M. (1965) Counting the poor: another look at the poverty profile. *Social Security Bulletin,* 28(1): 3–29.

U.S. Bureau of the Census (2017) *Measuring America: How the U.S. Census Bureau Measures Poverty.* Available from: https://www.census.gov/library/visualizations/2017/demo/poverty_measure-how.html

U.S. Department of Agriculture (2023) *Thrifty Food Plan, 2021.* Available from: https://www.fns.usda.gov/cnpp/usda-food-plans-cost-food-reports.

U.S. Department of Agriculture (2023) *Food Prices and Spending.* Available from: https://www.ers.usda.gov/data-products/ag-and-food-statistics-charting-the-essentials/food-prices-and-spending/#:~:text=Food%2Dat%2Dhome%20spending%20increased,to%20%241.34%20trillion%20in%202022

PART IV

Health and healthcare

TEN

Reproductive health in crisis: access to abortion and contraception in the US

Kristen Lagasse Burke and Dana M. Johnson

The problem

There is an abortion and contraceptive access crisis in the United States (US). On June 24, 2022, the US Supreme Court revoked the right to abortion in the landmark decision, *Dobbs v. Jackson Women's Health Organization (Dobbs)*, a ruling that overturned the Court's 1973 decision in *Roe v. Wade* and sent the issue of abortion legality back to the states.

Since the *Dobbs* ruling a cascade of abortion restrictions have been implemented. As of October 2023, 15 states have banned abortion with limited (and often not observed) exceptions. In 18 states, access is severely restricted due to gestational limits, waiting periods, lack of insurance coverage, or parental notification laws. These restrictions have ripple effects that go far beyond access to abortion care. State legislatures and conservative Judges are advocating for restrictions on contraception, gender-affirming care, and postpartum Medicaid. For health care seekers, providers, and advocates, the confusion, fear, and legal ambiguity following *Dobbs* has resulted in widespread chilling effects that have permeated the provision of reproductive health care.

As we address this current moment in history where access has been suddenly curtailed and the policy landscape remains volatile, it is important to note how legal restrictions on reproductive bodily autonomy—the freedom to decide if, when, and how to have a child and the liberation to shape these circumstances—have historically been used to oppress and control people with the capacity for pregnancy (including women, transgender men, gender expansive, and non-binary people). Historical context is imperative because it lays the groundwork for our understanding of the systems of structural and individual-level ableism, classism, sexism, and racism that shape disparities in health access and the contours of reproductive care in the contemporary US. These disparities are the result of policies—both past and present.

For over 250 years, slavery was legal in the US. Under this system, the US economy had a vested interest in controlling the childbearing of Black people. Although emancipation put a legal end to slavery, this legacy persisted through the eugenics movement and has resulted in racism embedded in reproductive medicine and policies. By the early 1900s, eugenicist theories claiming that people should shape the genetics and demographics of the population through selective procreating became increasingly supported by the US government. In the 1927 US Supreme Court decision *Buck v. Bell*, the court legitimized eugenic sterilization, and soon after, depopulation policies emerged. Between the 1920s and the 1970s, tens of thousands of people in the US and Puerto Rico were involuntarily sterilized by government family planning programs. For decades, the US government supported reproductive coercion programs, involuntary clinical trials, and family separation policies. These policies were primarily aimed at communities of color, immigrant communities, those with low incomes, and minors—the very same communities that shoulder the burden of today's bans on abortion and contraception.

In this chapter, we focus on the lack of access to abortion and contraception. Legal restrictions and inequalities in access that prevent people from choosing abortion or contraception, and thus the ability to control whether or not to bear children, represent a fundamental reproductive injustice that have implications for health and well-being across the lifespan.

Research evidence

Contraception and abortion are commonly used, safe components of healthcare that allow people to plan, space, and prevent births. According to the National Center for Health Statistics, contraceptive use is virtually universal among women of reproductive age in the US, with 99 percent of those aged 15–44 with sexual experience reporting that they have ever used a method. Further, nearly one in four women in the US will have an abortion by age 45. Although some methods are riskier for people with underlying health conditions, in general, contraception is extremely safe, and obtaining an abortion, whether by procedure or medication, results in complications less frequently than other common procedures like a wisdom tooth extraction. Importantly, the medical risks from contraception and abortion are vastly lower than from the alternative of pregnancy and childbirth. Considering the significantly elevated maternal mortality rate in the US compared to other high-income nations, and with Black women experiencing a rate nearly three times that of White women, having the agency to prevent unwanted pregnancies and births can serve as one of many critical health interventions.

Beyond facilitating women's agency over their health outcomes, rigorous scientific studies have shown that access to these services helps people complete their education, achieve better socioeconomic outcomes, and have a greater likelihood of achieving their goals. In short, contraception and abortion are essential tools that offer people more control over their lives.

Given their prevalence, safety, and utility, it is no surprise that contraception and abortion enjoy widespread public support. Gallup polls have shown that, as most Americans use contraception, so too do they find it morally acceptable. In the wake of the *Dobbs* decision, support for abortion remains high, and dissatisfaction with abortion policies is at an all-time high.[1] In the last year, state-level ballot measures to proactively protect abortion, such as Ohio's Issue 1 measure in the 2023 election to enshrine the right to abortion in its Constitution, have universally resulted in favorable outcomes for those seeking to preserve or expand abortion access.

Despite widespread use and support, access to care has persistently been inequitable. After decades of incrementally mounting restrictions and legal challenges to limit abortion access, the *Dobbs* decision has exacerbated existing inequalities in access across the US. The states that have banned abortion are concentrated in the South and Midwest, where people are disproportionately Black, poor, and are subject to weak state safety net policies to support families. In the year following the *Dobbs* decision, at least 61 clinics mostly in the South and Midwest closed or stopped providing abortions.[2] Garnering the economic resources to travel to and pay for an abortion, in addition to incidental costs such as childcare and time off work, have consistently posed obstacles to care that disproportionately affect those with the fewest resources, and these obstacles have only grown as a result of the mounting geographic barriers to care post-*Dobbs*. In the face of economic and logistical barriers to obtaining in-clinic abortion care, self-managed abortion using medication abortion pills can offer a more affordable option. However, some still find this unaffordable and inaccessible, and it is accompanied by legal risks.

The important role of contraception in supporting reproductive autonomy has only been elevated in the wake of *Dobbs*. Yet, contraceptive access is also riddled with longstanding challenges. The Guttmacher Institute estimates that there are nearly 50 million women of reproductive age seeking to prevent pregnancy in the US, and 21 million of them need publicly funded care due to their low income or young age. Most reside in counties that are considered "contraceptive deserts," where more than 1,000 women are in need of contraception per facility that provides the full range of methods.[3] Of those who wish to prevent pregnancy, one in five cannot access their desired method of contraception due to cost, and this experience is more common among Black and Hispanic women, younger women, and those living on low incomes. The persistent, overlapping inequities in access to abortion and contraception have resulted in the most marginalized people facing the greatest barriers to these two essential components of healthcare, and these barriers have only grown since *Roe* was overturned.

Recommendations and solutions

The burden of restrictive policies falls disproportionately on poor people, young people, and people of color; solutions to promote access to abortion and contraception should center these groups that have historically and currently been the most harmed. Policy is a valuable tool for advancing human rights and protecting people from harm. However, policy alone will not solve the current reproductive health care access crisis in the US. Community-based care and social justice movements have long advocated for and delivered health care services. As policy in the US has often fallen short, it is grassroots solutions that time and time again bring essential services to people in need. Therefore, in addition to advancing policy solutions, we also highlight several social justice and community-based priorities.

We categorize our recommendations at federal, state, and community levels. However, many of these policies and initiatives span multiple levels. We propose some recommendations as stopgap solutions to the current crisis, and others to restore access to abortion and contraception. Given the longstanding disparities in care, the current crisis in access poses an inflection point, from which we can seek not to restore the previous status quo, but to boldly envision a more inclusive future that supports people in achieving their reproductive desires.

Federal

- Codify the right to contraception

  At the federal and state levels, legislators should pass legislation that enshrines individuals' right to contraception, such as the Right to Contraception Act that was introduced in Congress.[4] The constitutional right to contraception was established under the 1965 Supreme Court decision in *Griswold v. Connecticut*, a decision that Justice Thomas suggested the court should reconsider in his concurring opinion on *Dobbs*. In reconsidering abortion rights, the Court has also opened the possibility for the right to contraception to be legally contested without such laws protecting access.

- Ensure affordability and accessibility of over-the-counter birth control

  In 2023, the FDA approved the first over-the-counter oral contraceptive medication. For this exciting development to meaningfully increase access to contraception, no-cost insurance coverage for the pill must be available without a prescription requirement, including for those who are covered by Medicaid, and the price point must be affordable for those without health insurance. Federal policies should address these concerns.

- Increase Title X funding

    The Title X program is the sole federal program dedicated to the provision of reproductive health services including contraceptive counseling and provision, STI testing and treatment, breast and cervical cancer screenings, and pregnancy testing (notably excluding abortion). This program primarily serves people who are uninsured and living on low incomes. Although tens of millions of people of reproductive age need publicly funded services, the budget of the Title X program has been held consistently at $286.5 million since 2014, an amount that can underwrite services for less than half of those in need. Increasing funding in the federal budget would support the expansion of the Title X network and the provision of services to a greater proportion of those in need.

- Repeal Comstock laws

    The Comstock laws were passed in 1873 to prohibit using the US postal service to mail "obscene" materials. Contemporary anti-abortion advocates have advanced a reading of these laws to prohibit the shipment of medication abortion pills. Repealing the Comstock Act would remove this threat from abortion access nationwide.

- Repeal the Hyde Amendment

    The Hyde Amendment blocks federal funds from being used to pay for abortion outside of exceptions for rape, incest, or if pregnancy is determined to endanger the person's life. Since the Hyde Amendment was introduced in 1973, it has dramatically limited coverage of abortion under Medicaid and other federal programs. For over 40 years, it has been sponsored and supported by legislators who oppose abortion. It is not a permanent law, but rather has been attached as a temporary "rider" to the Congressional appropriations bill for the Department of Health and Human Services and has been renewed annually by Congress. In 2020, President Biden released a historic statement opposing the Hyde Amendment. Congress should move to repeal the Hyde Amendment and make abortion care fully accessible for people with federally funded insurance.

State

- Ensure protections for pregnant people from criminalization

    The criminal legal system has increasingly treated pregnancy-related issues as inherently criminal matters. This has resulted in arrest and incarceration that separates pregnant people from their children, communities, and families. It also isolates pregnant people, keeping them from accessing essential health care and, as a result, exacerbating poor maternal, fetal, and child health outcomes. Legislatively, we can protect pregnant people from criminalization by repealing state fetal protection laws used to criminalize pregnancy and expanding protections for pregnant people (such as HIPPA laws). Broadly, we can also work to address the racist and classist systems that enable these laws by decoupling health care from policing and surveillance.

- Expand Medicaid in the remaining ten states

  Under the Affordable Care Act, the federal government offered support for states to expand their Medicaid coverage for adults with low incomes up to 138 percent of the Federal Poverty Level. Ten states have failed to adopt this expansion in the last decade, leaving millions without health insurance coverage. Notably, these states are concentrated in the South, where access to abortion and contraception is also limited. Whether through state-level legislation or ballot measures, the expansion of Medicaid in the remaining states would provide insurance coverage and, with it, the possibility of accessing no-cost contraception for those who currently fall in "coverage gaps."

- Expand abortion provision by advanced practice clinicians

  Nurse practitioners, midwives, and physician assistants can safely provide abortion care, but some state laws only permit physicians to provide abortions. Expanding the legal provision of abortion care to advanced practice clinicians could expand the capacity of states where abortion is still legal to meet the increased demand for the procedure from people traveling from states in which abortion is banned or restricted.

- Ensure abortion access for minors

  Thirty-six states require parental involvement in a minor's decision to have an abortion. Twenty-one states require only parental consent, three of which require both parents to consent to the abortion. Six states require both parental notification and consent. Ten states only require parental notification. These laws severely restrict access to abortion for minors (people under 18 years old). To work around parental notification laws, minors may seek judicial bypass, a legal procedure that allows them to appear before a Judge to obtain approval from a court. While judicial bypass can help minors obtain a wanted abortion, the process itself is mentally taxing, time-consuming, and, at times, traumatizing. Repealing all parental involvement laws would open access for people of all ages who desire abortion care.

- Enact shield laws to protect providers in protective access states

  In response to the targeting of abortion care providers, seven states to date have enacted "shield laws." Broadly, these laws seek to protect abortion providers, helpers, and seekers who live in states where abortion remains legal from legal attacks from anti-abortion state actors. Shield laws are seen as a new proactive legal strategy for protecting abortion provision and are increasingly being proposed and expanded in states that are legally protective of abortion rights.

- Advance ballot measures to enshrine abortion in state constitutions

For decades, state and local level politics have shaped access to sexual and reproductive health care, and this has been accelerated now that the Supreme Court ruled that the right to abortion is up to the state to determine. Since the *Dobbs* decision, Ohio, California, Michigan, and Vermont have passed ballot measures that enshrine abortion protections in their constitutions. In Kentucky, Montana, and Kansas, voters have rejected ballot measures that limit abortion access or criminalize providers. Engaging in these types of local, responsive, and fast-paced opportunities is a way for advocates and voters to directly shape abortion access.

• Decriminalize self-managed abortion

Self-managed medication abortion, or obtaining and using medication abortion pills and managing an abortion outside of the formal health care setting without direct clinician supervision, has increased substantially in the United States. This process can be safe and effective when authentic medication is used, and people are well equipped with information and support for potential complications. However, punitive state responses now pose a significant threat to people who self-manage their abortion. Decriminalization operates on multiple levels. At the local level, district attorneys must refuse to investigate and prosecute people who are suspected of self-managing their abortion. At the state level, Nevada specifically must repeal their law explicitly banning self-managed abortion. Throughout the country, local and state actors must end the misapplication of criminal laws that have been used in the past to intimidate and arrest people who may have self-managed their abortion.

Community

• Combat voter suppression

The elevated influence of local actors on reproductive health policy highlights the importance of local political engagement through elections and advocacy. Organizing to fight voter suppression is essential to ensure voters can enact policies that align reproductive health policy with public opinion. For example, in November 2023, Ohioans introduced Issue 1, a citizen-led ballot measure that would protect reproductive freedom. Grassroots organizations, primarily led by women of color, worked across the state to educate, mobilize, and successfully pass Issue 1.[5]

• Support grassroots reproductive health organizations

Reproductive care is community care for the health of our society. Abortion funds are mutual aid organizations that provide direct financial support to people. They help fund the cost of abortion care, the cost of traveling to care, or both. There are over 100 local abortion funds operating throughout the US. Organizations like Emergency Contraception for Every Campus have established peer-to-peer networks to share resources, like emergency contraception, condoms, and pregnancy tests with those in need, especially in restrictive settings. Independent clinics and Title X programs directly provide reproductive care. People seeking to contribute their time to the fight for reproductive justice should look to these local funding and care-providing organizations that deeply understand the needs of their community. Those with access to resources must invest directly in these community-based solutions.

- Challenge stigma

  In everyday life, we can normalize the full spectrum of reproductive health care, including abortion and contraception, by dispelling myths, challenging stigmatizing beliefs, and intentionally using language to affirm reproductive health care as a human right. Organizations like We Testify exist to support people who have had abortions in sharing their experiences, particularly those who have been marginalized in mainstream reproductive rights movements, so that their stories can help to shift the narrative and combat stigma around this extremely common experience. Further, the #shoutyourabortion movement is one example of a social media campaign that created a platform for people to share their abortion stories. Engaging in storytelling and stigma-challenging work can ensure that our communities see reproductive care as normal and essential.

- Build cross-coalition movements

  The movements for disability, economic, environmental, immigrant, racial, and transgender justice are deeply intertwined with the fight for reproductive health, rights, and justice. Cross-coalition building initiatives organize beyond access to abortion and contraception and work for a world where people have the resources to live healthy and safe lives. Considering the fight for reproductive health access as aligned with other social movements bolsters support for policies such as raising the minimum wage, expanding the social safety net to support undocumented families, expanding the Child Tax Credit (CTC), providing subsidies for childcare and paid family leave, ending mass incarceration, and ensuring access to affordable housing and education, which will support people as they build the families they desire.

Engagement with the issue of access to contraception and abortion has never been more urgent, as *Dobbs* dramatically restricted abortion access, and contraception is increasingly a target of political attacks. Yet, we remain hopeful that the future holds the potential for radical change, particularly in light of the reality that there have never been more people with the capacity for pregnancy studying reproductive health access, serving as political representatives, acting as leaders in healthcare, and advocating for change. Through policy action, coalition building, and community support, we can pursue equitable and expanded access to contraception and abortion, thus contributing to an inclusive future that guarantees reproductive freedom for all.

Notes

[1] Brenan, M. (2023) Dissatisfaction with U.S. abortion policy hits another high. Gallup. Available from: https://news.gallup.com/poll/470279/dissatisfaction-abortion-policy-hits-high.aspx

[2] McCann, A. and Walker, A. S. (2023) One year, 61 clinics: how dobbs changed the abortion landscape. *The New York Times* [online], June 23. Available from: https://www.nytimes.com/interactive/2023/06/22/us/abortion-clinics-dobbs-roe-wade.html

[3] Power to Decide (2023) Contraceptive deserts. Power to Decide. Available from: https://powertodecide.org/what-we-do/contraceptive-deserts

[4] Right to Contraception Act, H.R. 8373, 117th Congress (2022). Available from: https://docs.house.gov/billsthisweek/20220718/BILLS-117HR8373IH.pdf

[5] Lee-Wallace, L. (2023) The Black women who fought for Ohio's historic abortion win. *Elle.* Available from: https://www.elle.com/culture/career-politics/a45876130/ohio-abortion-rights-amendment-2023/

Key resources

Burke, K. L., Potter, J. E., and White, K. (2020) Unsatisfied contraceptive preferences due to cost among women in the United States. *Contraception: X,* 2, 100032.

Foster, D. G. (2021) *The Turnaway Study: Ten Years, A Thousand Women, and the Consequences Of Having—Or Being Denied—An Abortion.* Simon and Schuster.

Frost, J. J., Zolna, M. R., Frohwirth, L. F., Douglas-Hall, A., Blades, N., Mueller, J. et al (2019) Publicly supported family planning services in the United States: Likely need, availability and impact, 2016. Guttmacher Institute. Available from: https://www.guttmacher.org/report/publicly-supported-FP-services-US-2016

Fuentes, L. (2023) Inequity in US abortion rights and access: the end of roe is deepening existing divides. Guttmacher Institute. Available from: https://www.guttmacher.org/2023/01/inequity-us-abortion-rights-and-access-end-roe-deepening-existing-divides

Gunja, M. Z., Gumas, E. D., and Williams, R. D. (2022) *The U.S. Maternal Mortality Crisis Continues to Worsen: An International Comparison.* The Commonwealth Fund.

Johnson, D. M., Madera, M., Gomperts, R., and Aiken, A. R. (2021) The economic context of pursuing online medication abortion in the United States. *SSM-Qualitative Research in Health,* 1, 100003.

Kozhimannil, K. B., Hassan, A., and Hardeman, R. R. (2022) Abortion access as a racial justice issue. *New England Journal of Medicine,* 387(17): 1537–39.

National Academies of Sciences, Engineering, and Medicine (2018) *The Safety and Quality of Abortion Care in the United States.* National Academies Press.

Roberts, D. (2014) *Killing the Black Body: Race, Reproduction, and the Meaning of Liberty*. Vintage.

Ross, L. J., Brownlee, S. L., Diallo, D. D., Rodriquez, L., and Roundtable, L. (2001) The 'SisterSong Collective': Women of color, reproductive health and human rights. *American Journal of Health Studies*, 17(2): 79–88.

ELEVEN

A bold policy agenda for improving immigrant healthcare access in the US

Tiffany D. Joseph and Meredith Van Natta

The problem

Immigrants are more likely to lack health coverage and adequate access to health care compared to US citizens. By immigrants, we refer to undocumented and documented non-citizens and first-generation immigrants who are naturalized citizens. A primary reason for this discrepancy is immigrants' continued exclusion from public policies. The most recent example is the historic 2010 Affordable Care Act, the provisions of which are only available to citizens and a specific group of documented immigrants. Since the 1970s, lawmakers have pursued public policies denying both undocumented and recently arrived authorized immigrants access to public benefits, which provide a social safety net for many US citizens. This social safety net includes access to public health coverage, food and housing assistance, and supplementary income for lower-income individuals. And because 79 percent of contemporary immigrants are people of color, this exclusion has racialized implications.[1] As immigrants have become more non-White, public policies have broadened the scope of immigrants' exclusion from the social safety net, especially healthcare access. Correspondingly, perceptions of immigrants' of color (non-) deservingness have often shaped these policy decisions.[2] The 1996 Personal Responsibility and Work Opportunity Act (PRWORA) established a 5-year residency bar for Lawful Permanent Residents (LPRs or green card holders), limiting their eligibility for public benefits. The Illegal Immigration Reform and Immigration Responsibility Act (IIRIRA), also passed in 1996, made both undocumented and documented immigrants more subject to deportation for minor infringements than before. These policies made immigrants of various legal statuses ineligible for subsidized health coverage in the landmark 2010 Affordable Care Act (ACA).[3] Despite increasing healthcare protections and extending health coverage access for many Americans, ACA provisions excluded millions of immigrants.

Together, diminished access to health coverage and intensified immigration enforcement have negatively affected immigrants' healthcare access. And these negative impacts extend to those in mixed-status families (which consist of family members with different legal statuses) and account for an estimated 22 million people.[4] Even when immigrants can access healthcare services, they face other barriers to proper care and have trouble navigating the complex US healthcare system. Onerous (re)enrollment procedures for health coverage and the unusual concept of the "primary care provider" as the gatekeeper to getting care prevent many from even entering the healthcare system. For those lucky enough to make it that far, language and cultural differences with providers may result in suboptimal care or discriminatory treatment.

These exclusionary conditions have also intensified immigrants' experiences of "medical legal violence"—whereby criminal law, aggressive immigration enforcement, and restrictive healthcare policies collide to criminalize immigrants in their everyday life. Medical legal violence constrains immigrants' healthcare access and makes them wary of obtaining healthcare services that they perceive as associated with government agencies.[5] Potential institutional surveillance and immigration enforcement through immigrants' contact with the healthcare system further undermine their healthcare access and complicate healthcare workers' efforts to provide care. These compounding challenges make it harder for immigrants to get the health care they need when they most need it. Therefore immigrants— especially immigrants of color who are disproportionately excluded and surveilled—constitute a large and important demographic to consider in making policy decisions that affect healthcare access in the US.

Research evidence

According to the Kaiser Family Foundation, in 2021, the uninsured rate among lawfully present immigrants was 25 percent, and 46 percent among undocumented immigrants, whereas only 8 percent of citizens were uninsured.[6] Aside from health policy exclusion, overlapping immigration and welfare policies indirectly affect immigrants' health and social service use. Notably, the public charge rule, which has been a part of immigration law for over a century, also aimed to limit immigrants' use of public benefits. This led to a "chilling effect" in which immigrants and immigrant families have disenrolled from or avoided social service use for which they are eligible.[7] The Trump administration's expansion of that rule in 2019 intensified that effect. The Biden administration has since nullified that change, but the detrimental impacts on immigrants' health care persist.[8] These impacts extend to citizen relatives in mixed-status families, who also fear enrolling in and using public health coverage because it could draw attention to undocumented relatives.

Explicitly racist and anti-immigrant rhetoric in recent years has further criminalized and scapegoated immigrants of color already within and who aim to traverse US borders.[9] But this is not new. Race and ethnicity have shaped immigration and other policies since the nation's founding, initially limiting citizenship access to White property-holding men.[10] Though constitutional amendments have broadened eligibility for citizenship since, current and previous waves of immigrants have been blamed for various societal ills: increases in crime, depressing workers' wages, and being carriers of disease. Indeed, historically it was within certain immigrant-serving clinics that racist immigration enforcement practices marked "non-White" immigrants as suspicious and un-deserving.[11]

While this legacy is long in the making, increasingly aggressive immigration enforcement activities within and beyond healthcare settings have heightened fear of detention and deportation in immigrant communities, particularly those of color.[12] Raids and threats of raids cause immigrants to stay home from work, not send their kids to school, avoid driving/public transportation, and forego medical treatment. Enforcement also undermines healthcare institutions' designation as "sensitive locations," where enforcement officials are theoretically prohibited from detaining immigrants.[13] However, numerous accounts of immigration enforcement officials waiting outside such sensitive locations have intensified the aforementioned chilling effect.

Recommendations and solutions

Federal reforms

Changes to health and immigration policy at the federal level are vital to improving immigrants' healthcare access. The most consequential policy change affecting both would be comprehensive immigration reform. Creating a path to legal permanent residency and citizenship would make more immigrants eligible for health coverage and other public benefits. Unfortunately, increasing political polarization and gridlock around immigration policy make such comprehensive reform unlikely. Despite these challenges, opportunities for policy reforms exist at multiple levels of governance. Here are our recommendations for federal-level policies:

- The U.S. Department of Health and Human Services (HHS) should increase: (1) the number, and ethnoracial and linguistic diversity, of healthcare navigators; (2) medical interpreter services; and (3) funding for diversifying the medical workforce. Such measures are essential to improving immigrants' health and healthcare access and ensuring compliance under Title VI of the 1964 Civil Rights Act, which prohibits programs receiving federal funds from discriminating on the basis of race, color, or national origin. (Language is a marker of national origin and consequently a protected status under Title VI.) For healthcare systems to be responsive to the unique needs of immigrant individuals and families, they should include more clinical and non-clinical personnel (such as health navigators, certified interpreters, and eligibility workers) who are representative of the communities they serve.

- Federal policies, such as those outlined in recent executive orders related to racial equity and immigrant integration, should continue to critically evaluate immigrant communities' unique needs in these areas and invest in strategies that ensure health care is accessible and compliant with federal law. For example, Executive Order 13985 aims to advance racial equity and support underserved communities by identifying and addressing systemic barriers to benefits in federal programs.[14] Executive Order 14012 seeks to restore faith in the immigration system and immigrant integration by reviewing and improving existing policies across multiple agencies.[15]

- States that have not yet expanded Medicaid under the 2010 ACA should do so without delay. Medicaid coverage reduces the overall number of uninsured individuals, enabling more people to access essential care services and avoid costly, uncompensated care. While many immigrants are ineligible to receive Medicaid services directly, expanded Medicaid coverage eases overall strain on states' healthcare safety net institutions. Arizona is one example of a state that expanded Medicaid within an otherwise immigrant-exclusionary political context, on the premise that doing so would benefit everyone in the state—particularly US citizens.[16] Whatever the political logic, reducing rates of uninsurance and uncompensated care can help remove barriers to health care and improve health equity for all residents regardless of immigration status.

State and local reforms

Amid current bipartisan gridlock in Congress and little appetite to prioritize the healthcare access of immigrants on either side of the political aisle, action has shifted to the state, county, and municipal level. While some states like Florida and Texas have implemented harsher policies to criminalize and exclude immigrants from health care, others have used state funding to extend access to health care for immigrants in their jurisdictions. We recommend other states follow the lead of these more inclusive, less punitive jurisdictions.

- California recently expanded its Medicaid program ("Medi-Cal") to income-eligible immigrants who are ineligible for federal Medicaid coverage. Children, young adults under 26, and adults aged 50 and over are already eligible for Medi-Cal, and California residents aged 26–49 will be eligible in January 2024.

- Massachusetts has the Health Safety Net program, which uses state funds to support the primary healthcare needs of income-eligible state residents over age 19 regardless of documentation status.
- Several states—including California, Connecticut, Illinois, New Jersey, New York, Oregon, Washington State, and the District of Columbia—provide publicly funded health care for undocumented immigrant children under the age of 18.
- Some states also provide programs for specific groups of undocumented immigrant adults. From 2020 to 2023, for example, Illinois offered public health insurance that was like Medicaid to immigrants aged 42 and older who met specific income eligibility thresholds and who were either undocumented or had been a legal permanent resident for less than 5 years (the minimum residency period required to qualify for federal Medicaid). Some states, such as Alaska, California, and Hawaii, have also offered more expansive coverage to certain federally unqualified immigrants for specific medical conditions, such as cancer or end-stage renal disease.
- Beyond statewide policies, counties and cities could further improve immigrant health by allocating local funding to provide preventive and other health services to immigrants. Programs like Healthy San Francisco and My Health LA have done this for residents not yet eligible for Medi-Cal. In a more restrictive state policy context such as in Texas, counties like Harris County (which includes the city of Houston) and municipalities like the city of San Antonio, provide a limited range of non-acute dialysis services for otherwise unqualified immigrants.
- Local jurisdictions can also provide more assistance to apply for coverage and offer health and social services in multiple languages for a very diverse population. Local departments of public health, Federally Qualified Health Centers (FQHCs), and Community Health Centers (CHCs) can identify specific community needs related to legal status, language access, and cultural practices and develop targeted outreach and enrollment strategies to insure healthcare access for immigrants.
- Finally, state and local jurisdictions can mitigate punitive federal immigration laws by enacting inclusive policies that promote trust and security in immigrant communities. This includes pursuing "sanctuary" policies that limit state, county, and municipal agencies' participation in immigration enforcement activities and enabling residents to obtain a state driver's license regardless of their legal status. For example, the 2017 California Values Act limits the involvement of California police and sheriffs in federal immigration enforcement activities and restricts these activities at various sensitive locations, including public schools, courthouses, and healthcare institutions. Such policies would reduce immigrants' deportation fears and make them more comfortable obtaining health care.

Reforms within healthcare institutions, agencies, and community organizations

In addition to state and local policy-making, the connections between healthcare institutions and legal aid and immigrant advocacy organizations should be strengthened to bridge policy gaps and improve protections for immigrant individuals and families seeking health care.

- Healthcare institutions should promote immigrant-inclusive messaging and practices to reassure community members that their primary aim is to provide care, not police the community. Resources for such messaging can be found at the Protecting Families Coalition.[17] This will help combat rising fears of immigration enforcement associated with the use of safety-net resources.
- Healthcare facilities should work with immigrant rights organizations to host "Know Your Rights" trainings, which instruct immigrant individuals and families about their rights and provide guidance on responding to situations ranging from employment and education challenges to immigration and law enforcement encounters. Such trainings should include distribution of red cards from the Immigrant Legal Resource Center (ILRC), an organization that advocates for immigrant rights. These red cards are available in more than a dozen languages and include emergency instructions for law and/ or immigration enforcement encounters. They can be ordered or printed from this website: https://www.ilrc.org/red-cards.
- Healthcare systems should also develop protocols for managing immigration enforcement in clinical spaces. These procedures include designating specific personnel to liaise with immigration enforcement officials, training staff to interpret warrants, and leveraging laws that protect patient privacy, such as the 1996 Health Insurance Portability and Accountability Act (HIPAA) and constitutional amendments related to privacy and due process. In 2019, for example, healthcare facilities associated with the University of California system integrated many of these strategies in an institutional policy entitled "Responding to Immigration Enforcement Issues Involving Patients in UC Health Facilities."

Political mobilization

Coordinated political organizing at the federal and state level can also dismantle anti-immigrant policies and promote more equitable health care for immigrant communities.

- Immigrants, concerned allies, and national organizations like the National Immigration Law Center (NILC) have been at the forefront of advocating for and demanding the implementation of humane policies and treatment for immigrants at the federal level.

- Similarly, at the state level, broad-based immigrant rights movements have challenged anti-immigrant laws. For example, grassroots organizing in states with a history of anti-immigrant policies like Arizona and Georgia has successfully engaged civic participation to advocate against inequitable social policies—particularly in communities of color in areas governed by conservative lawmakers. Even states with more inclusive current policies, such as California, owe such progress largely to the efforts of immigrant and civil rights activists in the 1990s who successfully overturned the state's anti-immigrant Proposition 187, which excluded many immigrants from a variety of public benefits. Ongoing mobilization and litigation have since led to one of the most immigrant-inclusive state safety nets in the country.

- These organizing efforts emphasize immigrants' important contributions to their communities, assert their rights to health and safety, and pressure lawmakers to enact more just social policies.

As we look ahead toward possible solutions to improve immigrants' healthcare access as a fundamental strategy for promoting US health equity, we must also reckon with the enduring and recent disparities that inequitable public policies have wrought. The COVID-19 pandemic has revealed that longstanding restrictions on immigrant eligibility for vital health services are arbitrary and unjustified. While many immigrant and mixed-status families were ineligible for economic stimulus support and unemployment insurance, efforts to protect public health removed legal status barriers for services such as COVID testing, vaccination, and other COVID-specific needs. That such health care *can* be administered without reference to legal status begs the question of why this is only the case under emergency conditions. The pandemic revealed the interconnectedness of community members' health and well-being and emphasized that no one benefits from an inequitable healthcare landscape. While the immediate public health emergency designation has ended, we must acknowledge persisting inequities and look ahead to proactively address them before immigrants' health is further harmed. Researchers should also examine the impact of inclusive COVID measures on healthcare access as evidence to bolster lawmakers' support for making such measures permanent.

The policies that exclude immigrants and their families from health care are not inevitable. These policies are a political choice that reflects enduring, racialized notions of deservingness that regard many immigrants (and some citizens) with suspicion despite their essential contributions to the social and economic fabric of US society. As we have described here, audacious policy change is possible at multiple levels of governance and is already yielding positive changes in specific jurisdictions and institutions. By learning from these successes and continuing to identify and dismantle the discrimination that constrains immigrants' healthcare access, we can effectively pursue more equitable and just approaches in the future.

Notes

[1] Ward and Batalova (2023).

[2] Hero, R. and R. Preuhs. (2007) Immigration and the evolving American welfare state: examining policies in the U.S. states. *American Journal of Political Science*, 51(3): 498–517.

[3] Joseph, T. (2016) What healthcare reform means for immigrants: a comparison of the affordable care act and Massachusetts health reforms. *Journal of Health Policy, Politics, and Law*, 41(1): 101–16.

[4] Connor, P. (2021) Immigration reform can keep millions of mixed-status families together. Fwd.us. Available from: https://www.fwd.us/news/mixed-status-families/

[5] Van Natta, M. (2023) *Medical Legal Violence: Health Care and Immigration Enforcement Against Latinx Noncitizens*. New York University Press.

[6] Kaiser Family Foundation (2022).

[7] "Chilling effect" is a term that scholars have developed to account for individuals disenrolling from or being reluctant to enroll in publicly funded social services due to changes in policy and immigration enforcement activities, sociopolitical climate, or eligibility rules. See: Watson, T. (2014) Inside the refrigerator: immigration enforement and chilling effects in Medicaid participation. *American Economic Journal: Economic Policy*, 6(3): 313–38.

[8] Beier, J. and Workie, E. (2022). The public-charge final rule is far from the last word. Available from: https://www.migrationpolicy.org/news/public-cha rge-final-rule-far-last-word

[9] Allen, C. (2022) The cruel public health consequences of anti-immigrant rhetoric. *American Journal of Public Health*, 112(12): 1726–8.

[10] Ngai, M. (2007) Birthright citizenship and the alien citizen. *Fordham Law Review*, 75: 2521–3295.

[11] Ong, A. (2003) *Buddha is Hiding: Refugees, Citizenship, The New America*. University of California Press.

[12] Artiga, S. and Ubri, P. (2017) Living in an immigrant family in America: How fear and toxic stress are affecting daily life, well-being, & health. Kaiser Family Foundation. Available from: https://www.kff.org/racial-equity-and-health-policy/issue-brief/liv ing-in-an-immigrant-family-in-america-how-fear-and-toxic-stress-are-affecting-daily- life-well-being-health/

[13] According to the Department of Homeland Security, "sensitive locations" are locations where immigration enforcement is not allowed, such as schools, healthcare facilities, and places of worship. See: Department of Homeland Security (2021) Guidelines for enforcement actions in or near protected areas memo. Available from: https://www.dhs. gov/publication/guidelines-enforcement-actions-or-near-protected-areas-memo.

[14] The White House (2021a) Executive order on advancing racial equity and support for underserved communities through the federal government. Available from: https://www. whitehouse.gov/briefing-room/presidential-actions/2021/01/20/executive-order-advanc ing-racial-equity-and-support-for-underserved-communities-through-the-federal-gov ernment/.

[15] The White House (2021b) Executive order on restoring faith in our legal immigration systems and strengthening integration and inclusion efforts for new Americans. Available

from: https://www.whitehouse.gov/briefing-room/presidential-actions/2021/02/02/executive-order-restoring-faith-in-our-legal-immigration-systems-and-strengthening-integration-and-inclusion-efforts-for-new-americans/.

[16] Castaneda, H. (2018) Stratification by immigration status: contradictory exclusion and inclusion after health care reform. In J. M. Mulligan and H. Castañeda (Eds) *Unequal Coverage: The Experience of Health Care Reform in the United States.* New York University Press, 37–58.

[17] See the following link for healthcare providers: https://pifcoalition.org/find-resources.

Key resources

Bitler, M., Hoynes, H., and Schanzenbach, D. (2020) The social safety net in the wake of COVID-19. *Brookings Papers on Economic Activity*, 2: 119–45.

Budd, K.M. and Bersani, B.E. (2020) Crimmigration: the presumption of illegality and the criminalization of immigrants. In G. Muschert, K. Budd, M. Christian, and R. Perrucci (Eds), *Agenda for Social Justice 2020*, Policy Press, 105–13.

Bulanda, J. and Pittman, A. (2020) In pursuit of justice in U.S. health care policy: pathways to universal coverage. In G. Muschert, K. Budd, M. Christian, and R. Perrucci (Eds), *Agenda for Social Justice 2020*, Policy Press, 43–51.

Faculti (2023) Medical legal violence [Video]. Available from: https://faculti.net/medical-legal-violence/

Gelatt, J. and Chishti, M. (2022) COVID-19's effects on U.S. immigration and immigrant communities, two years on. Migration Policy Institute. Available from: https://www.migrationpolicy.org/research/covid19-effects-us-immigration

Joseph, T., and Golash-Boza, T. (2021) Double consciousness in the 21st century: Du Boisian theory and the problem of racialized legal status. *Social Sciences*, 10(9): 345.

Kaiser Family Foundation (2022) Health coverage and care of immigrants. Available from: https://www.kff.org/racial-equity-and-health-policy/fact-sheet/health-coverage-and-care-of-immigrants/

Sugrue, N. and Puente, S. (2020) Latinos are each of us: fair and just immigration policies for all. In G. Muschert, K. Budd, M. Christian, and R. Perrucci (Eds.), *Agenda for Social Justice 2020*, Policy Press, 13–20.

Ward, N. and Batalova, J. (2023) *Frequently Requested Statistics on Immigrants and Immigration in the United States.* Migration Policy Institute. Available from: https://www.migrationpolicy.org/article/frequently-requested-statistics-immigrants-and-immigration-united-states#:~:text=In%202021%2C%20immigrants%20comprised%2013.6,share%20they%20comprised%20in%202019

TWELVE

Gender-affirming healthcare for transgender and gender minority youth

Ashley C. Rondini

The problem

Extensive evidence-based research demonstrates the positive impact of gender-affirming care on health outcomes for gender minority youth, as invoked repeatedly in statements of support and advocacy by professional medical associations in the United States and beyond. Yet, in recent years, gender-affirming healthcare for gender minority youth in the US has been made the target of disinformation campaigns, inflammatory political rhetoric, and conservative legislative restrictions, judicial precedents, and/or executive actions by state, district, and local governments. The potential harm posed by these political attacks is significant in scope. Of approximately 1.6 million transgender Americans, more than 300,000 are under 17 years old.[1]

Gender-affirming healthcare is resoundingly supported as the highest standard of evidence-based practice in treating transgender, gender diverse, non-binary, and intersex youth (collectively referred to here as "gender minority youth") by the World Health Organization (WHO), the American Medical Association (AMA), the American Association of Medical Colleges (AAMC), the American Public Health Association (APHA), American Academy of Child and Adolescent Psychiatry (AACAP) the American Psychiatric Association (APA), the American College of Physicians (ACP), the Endocrine Society, and the American Academy of Pediatrics (AAP), among others.

Holistic approaches to gender-affirming care center on mental and physical wellness for gender minority youth as they navigate their adolescence in the context of a transphobic society. Social affirmation (support for the use of names, pronouns, markers of physical appearance, and safe access to social groupings, activities, and facilities congruent with one's gender identity) is considered the most fundamental form of gender-affirming care for patients at any developmental stage or age. Additional modalities of gender-affirming care may be considered on an individual basis at age-appropriate stages in a patient's physical and psychological development, in consultation with a team of care providers. These may include puberty blockers (administered after the onset of puberty to delay the development of secondary sex characteristics), hormonal therapy (estrogen administered for transfeminine patients and testosterone administered for transmasculine patients, after the age of 16), "top" (chest) surgery (after the age of 16), voluntary hysterectomies (after the age of 18) and gender affirmation genital surgery (after the age of 18).[2] Surgical interventions are the least commonly utilized form of gender-affirming healthcare overall, and particularly for adolescents. Consideration for hysterectomy procedures or genital surgery is extraordinarily rare for patients under the age of 18.[3]

Gender minority youth experience heightened levels of childhood trauma exposure as a consequence of their disproportionate victimization to in-school bullying, harassment, physical and sexual violence, abuse,[4] overall lack of social supports, social marginalization, higher degrees of familial estrangement, and—consequent to the latter—risks of homelessness.[5] Owing to these social factors, gender minority youth experience disparate overall health outcomes and heightened risk of adverse mental health outcomes including depression, self-harm, substance abuse, and suicide. Yet, scholarship also demonstrates that overall well-being and experiences of joy are increased for transgender individuals who have the opportunity to safely embrace and express their identities, despite the marginalization that they face.[6] The provision of gender-affirming healthcare, unsurprisingly, has been shown to substantially mitigate adverse mental health outcomes such as depression, anxiety, and suicidality for this population, despite the persistent socio-structural risk factors that remain.

Research evidence

In 2022, after bans on gender-affirming healthcare for transgender youth were passed in Texas, Alabama, and Florida, a cross-disciplinary team of experts collaborated on two rebuttal papers combatting the scientific disinformation—that is, intentionally misleading falsehoods presented as scientific fact—upon which legal arguments had been scaffolded to undergird the new legal restrictions. These experts—representing adolescent medicine, child and adolescent psychiatry, pediatric endocrinology, psychology, and law—debunked false claims that had challenged the scientific verifiability of evidence supporting gender-affirming care, asserted the mental health benefits of gender affirming care, cautioned against the mental health consequences of denying gender-affirming care, and pointed out the use of misleading terminology that had been used to introduce and advocate for the bans. As political vitriol continues to supplant medical expertise in adjudicating access to healthcare, providers are being legally required to violate their own professional code of ethics, to "do no harm"—with potentially catastrophic consequences for the well-being and safety of an already underserved and widely persecuted population.

By March of 2023, over 450 anti-LGBTQ+ bills that had been already been proposed in state legislatures[7] and 156,500 gender minority youth lived in 32 states where access to gender-affirming care had been restricted or was at risk of being banned.[8] Beyond their direct impact on access to services, these bills heighten fear and stigma for young people, who experience increased distress and mental health concerns in the context of an increasingly hostile socio-political environment. Further, 94 percent of LGBTQ+ youth report negative mental health outcomes related to recent politics.[9]

Also in March of 2023, Rep. Marjorie Taylor Greene (GA-14) introduced H.R. 1399, "to prohibit gender-affirming care on minors, and for other purposes." Shortly thereafter, Rep. Jayapal Pramila (D-WA-17) introduced a contrary resolution H. Res 269, "Recognizing that it is the duty of the Federal Government to develop and implement a Transgender Bill of Rights to protect and codify the rights of transgender and non-binary people under the law and ensure their access to medical care, shelter, safety, and economic security." Although neither bill has passed as of this writing, the introduction of the former clearly demonstrates the urgent need for the latter.

On July 27, 2023, lawmakers in the House of Representatives Judiciary Committee's Subcommittee on the Constitution and Limited Government held a hearing titled "The Dangers and Due Process Violations of 'Gender-Affirming' Care for Children." At the hearing, Committee Chairman Mike Johnson (R, LA) used inflammatory language to characterize any and all forms of gender-affirming care as tantamount to "forcing" involuntary genital surgery on children in acts of "barbarism" and "mutilation" that would "permanently change their bodies." This fear-mongering rhetoric, rife with disinformation, is ostensibly being deployed to invoke a collective sense of moral outrage at the idea of children being "endangered." In actual fact, gender minority youth are endangered by the stigmatization that such language amplifies,[10] and the barriers to safely accessible healthcare that the hearing was intended to legitimize.

In May of 2022, the non-partisan Pew Research Center conducted a survey of Americans' views regarding gender identity and transgender issues. The findings of this report revealed, among other insights, that views on these issues remain divided such that protections for LGBTQ+ youth health and healthcare are far from assured;

- 41 percent of Americans support the implementation of policies requiring transgender individuals to use public restrooms that match the sex that they were assigned at birth, while 31 percent oppose such measures, and 28 percent neither support nor oppose them.

- 37 percent of Americans support investigating parents for child abuse if they help someone under the age of 18 get medical care related to gender transition, while 36 percent oppose such measures, and 27 percent neither support nor oppose them.
- 46 percent of Americans support making it illegal for health care professionals to help someone under the age of 18 with medical care related to gender transition, while 31 percent oppose such measures, and 22 percent neither support nor oppose them.[11]

While the political momentum behind anti-transgender legislative initiatives seems to be finding purchase among a wider base of American voters, the possible threat of federal legislation—either directly restricting access to gender-affirming care or protecting states' rights to do so—looms large in the upcoming election cycle. This was evidenced early on by the heated debates concerning gender-affirming care that comprised a portion of the Republican presidential primary debates in December of 2023.

Recommendations and solutions

A holistic and multi-pronged approach to creating protections for gender-affirming care must be undertaken to combat the political and legal attacks that currently threaten (and, in some states, already restrict) patient access. As detailed next, this approach must account for the variety of legal mechanisms, legislative initiatives, and political disinformation campaigns currently targeting transgender, non-binary, gender diverse, and intersex youth, their families, their supporters, and their healthcare providers. To be effective, approaches towards future solutions must be contextualized by the recent history of efforts to ban gender-affirming care, and formulate strategies that anticipate the ongoing implications of the socio-political landscape that such efforts have created.

Background to policy recommendations

Under the purview of the Department of Health and Human Services Office of Civil Rights, Section 1557 of the Patient Protection and Affordable Care Act (42 U.S.C. 18116) on Non-Discrimination in Health Programs and Activities prohibits "discrimination on the basis of race, color, national origin, age, disability, or sex (including pregnancy, sexual orientation, gender identity, and sex characteristics)" in any health-related programs receiving federal financial assistance in the form of credits, subsidies, or insurance contracts, as well as any program or activity "administered by an Executive Agency, or any entity established under Title I of the ACA or its amendments" (42 U.S.C. 18116).

Yet, in February of 2022, Texas Attorney General Ken Paxton issued a legal opinion that equated gender-affirming care for transgender youth with "child abuse." This opinion stated that anyone who had "reasonable cause" to believe that such "abuse" was taking place was legally obligated to report it within 48 hours or be charged with a criminal offense under a Texas "family code" which criminalizes complicity with child abuse. In March of 2022, Texas Governor Gregg Abbott signed an executive order directing the state's Department of Family and Protective Services (DFPS) to investigate the parents of any transgender children or teens for child abuse.

In response, also in March of 2022, the Department of Health and Human Services issued "HHS Notice and Guidance on Gender Affirming Care, Civil Rights, and Patient Privacy." In the notice, the HHS cited Section 1557 of the Patient Protection and Affordable Care Act, and took the position that (a) healthcare providers subject to unlawful restrictions on providing gender-affirming care to their patients can file grievances with the HHS Office of Civil Rights, and that (b) families experiencing healthcare discrimination on the basis of their child's gender identity or gender expression have the right to file grievances with the HHS Office of Civil Rights.[12] However, in October of 2022, the District Court of Northern Texas issued a judgment that vacated the March 2022 HHS document. At the time of this writing, the HHS document is still available online, with a brief statement added at its top noting the decision and stating that HHS is "evaluating its next steps in light of that judgment but is complying with it." This ruling opened the political floodgates for a rash of local- and state-level bills restricting or prohibiting the provision of gender-affirming care throughout the country since that time.

By August of 2023, 142 bills had been introduced in state legislatures focused on restricting access to gender-affirming healthcare, with 117 focused specifically on restricting gender affirming care for minors, through a variety of legal mechanisms. For example:

- 76 bills proposed in state legislatures in 2023 would revoke the medical licenses of healthcare providers offering gender-affirming care to their patients.
- 27 of these proposed bills would criminalize gender-affirming care, attaching felony charges to either the healthcare provider offering care, the patient seeking care, a social worker or mental healthcare provider advocating or supporting care, or the parents of the patient seeking care on behalf of minor children.
- 27 of these bills seek to ban Medicaid or other publicly funded health plans, such as Veteran's Administration health insurance, from covering gender-affirming care.[13]

In light of this context, comprehensive efforts to safeguard gender-affirming care for gender minority youth must address the following concerns:

Leverage expert knowledge of LGBTQ+ youth healthcare providers in educating policy makers at the local, state, and federal level

- Parents, families, and allies of LGBTQ+ youth should seek out medical guidance and advocacy strategies regarding the health of gender minority youth that is sourced from credible medical providers in the field, with established expertise in gender-affirming care.

  In recent years, an increasing number of leading children's hospitals and pediatric care centers have developed programs and services to specifically support the mental and physical health, overall well-being, and safety of LGBTQ+ youth. Some, like the Gender and Sexuality Development Program at Children's Hospital of Philadelphia, have educational advocates on staff to work with school districts, educational institutions, and individual families to achieve the affirming and inclusive implementation of policies, development of curricula, and equitable provision of educational resources and opportunities for LGBTQ+ students.

Establish federal protections for the civil rights of transgender, non-binary, and gender minority people

- Pass House Resolution 269 into law

  "Recognizing that it is the duty of the Federal Government to develop and implement a Transgender Bill of Rights to protect and codify the rights of transgender and non-binary people under the law and ensure their access to medical care, shelter, safety, and economic security."
- Pass amendments to explicitly add "gender identity" as a protected category within existing Federal anti-discrimination legislation that could be relevant to the health/well-being, safety, or health insurance bearing on access to gender-affirming care for gender minority youth.

  This could include, but would not be limited to, Title IX of the 1972 Education Amendments (prohibiting discrimination on the basis of sex) to account for social affirmation and inclusive access to educational activities and sports[14] in schools as well as direct provision health services in school-based clinics, Title VI of the Civil Rights Act of 1964 (prohibiting discrimination in public programs) to account for means-tested programs such as Medicaid as well as VA health insurance benefits for veterans and their dependents, and Title VII of the Civil Rights of 1964 (prohibiting employment discrimination) to account for employer based medical insurance, and the Civil Rights Act of 1968 (prohibiting housing discrimination) to account for issues of safety and security and access to neighborhood public health facilities and clinics.

Establish federal regulations to prevent the political weaponization of "child abuse" charges and misuse of social service system resources for political purposes

- Provide sustained federal legal protections for parents and guardians of gender minority youth seeking gender-affirming care for the children in their care.

  Federal protections are needed to shield families from politically weaponized charges of "child abuse" in states and municipalities that have implemented such intimidation tactics to discourage families from putting supports in place for their children.

- Amend the Child Abuse Prevention and Treatment Act (CAPTA) (42 U.S.C.A. § 5106g) to specify that seeking evidence-based medical treatment endorsed as best practice by professional medical associations and established expert consensus does not constitute child abuse.

  Presently, the CAPTA Reauthorization Act of 2010 defines child abuse and neglect by a parent or caregiver as, "Any recent act or failure to act on the part of a parent or caretaker which results in death, serious physical or emotional harm, sexual abuse or exploitation;" or "An act or failure to act which presents an imminent risk of serious harm." The House Committee on Education and Labor, as the committee that introduced the original CAPTA bill and its subsequent reauthorizations, must propose a federal guideline that explicitly specifies protection against falsified child abuse charges when a parent or caretaker is seeking appropriate medical care for a minor child. Such an amendment at the federal level would safeguard families against the politically weaponized appropriation of the term "child abuse"—as well as the consequences of the term being misused and redefined in policy—across all states.

- Establish financial penalties for states that systematically misallocate social service system resources for the investigation of "child abuse" charges when the conduct at issue is actually evidence-based medical treatment endorsed as best practice by professional medical associations and established expert consensus.

- Provide legal recourse through civil processes (financial compensation) and legal accountability through criminal charges against politicians who level false accusations (slander) and legislate investigations (harassment, intimidation) of "child abuse" against parents and healthcare providers of gender minority youth.

Protect healthcare providers that offer gender-affirming care

- Provide federal protection from local legislative interference and/or legal censure for all medical facilities and individual providers offering affirming and holistic care to gender minority youth that is consistent with the evidence-based best practices established by the American Academy of Pediatrics (AAP) and all of the previously listed professional medical and healthcare organizations.

At the AAP's 2023 Annual Leadership Conference, organization voters resolved to prioritize advocacy for gender-affirming care as a human right and advocacy for federal protections of gender affirming care for both patients and their doctors. Both the professional standings and legal standings of healthcare providers must be protected.

Provide sustained federal protections for gender minority youth by codifying their access to healthcare in safe and affirming environments

- Codify protection against discrimination on the basis of "gender identity and gender expression" in healthcare as an independent category rather than a subcategory or sex discrimination.

  The inclusion of "gender identity" discrimination as a form of sex discrimination under Section 1557 of the Affordable Care and Patient Privacy Act was an important step in the direction of codifying anti-discrimination protections, but the current status of that protection is dubious in light of the Northern District of Texas ruling in October of 2022. While HHS presently maintains the position that gender identity is encompassed by civil rights protections under "sex," leaving the explicit, independent language of "gender identity and gender expression" as its own category out of the statute leaves the legality of these federal protection mandates open to varying judicial interpretation. Codifying explicit protections for healthcare access without discrimination on the basis of gender identity and gender expression—not as part of sex discrimination, but as an explicitly protected category unto itself—is therefore critically important.

Acknowledgments

I am indebted to David Woods, JD, Jonathan Peck, JD, Maria del Carmen Flores, JD, and Madeleine Peck Wagner, MFA, for their thoughtful reviews of this chapter.

Notes

[1] Redfield et al (2023).

[2] Boerner (2022).

[3] Respaut, R. and Terhune, C. (2022) Number of transgender children seeking treatment surges in U.S. *Reuters.* Available from: https://www.reuters.com/article/usa-transyouth-data-idUKL1N3142UU

[4] Martín-Castillo, D., Jiménez-Barbero, J. A., del Mar Pastro-Bravo, M., Sánchez-Muñoz, M., Elvira Fernández-Espín, M., and Joaquín García-Arenas, J. (2020) School victimization in transgender people: a systematic review. *Children and Youth Services Review*, 119: 10580.

[5] The National Child Traumatic Stress Network (n.d.) Gender affirming care is trauma-informed care. Available from: https://www.nctsn.org/sites/default/files/resources/fact-sheet/gender-affirming-care-is-trauma-informed-care.pdf

[6] Shuster, S. M. and Westbrook, L. (2022) Reducing the joy deficit in sociology: a study of transgender joy. *Social Problems*: spac034. Available from: https://doi.org/10.1093/socpro/spac034

[7] American Civil Liberties Union (ACLU) (2023) Mapping attacks on LGBTQ rights in U.S. state legislatures. Available from: https://www.aclu.org/legislative-attacks-on-lgbtq-rights?impact=health.

[8] See note 1.

[9] The Trevor Project (2021) "National survey on LGBTQ youth mental health 2021. Available from: https://www.thetrevorproject.org/survey2021/?section=SupportingTransgenderNonbinaryYouth

[10] Kota, K. K., Salazar, L. F., Culbreth, R. E., Crosby, R. A., and Jones, J. (2020) Psychosocial mediators of perceived stigma and suicidal ideation among transgender women. *BMC Public Health*, 20: 125.

[11] Parker, K., Horowitz, J. M., and Brown, A. (2022) Americans' complex views on gender identity and transgender issues. Pew Research Center. Available from: https://www.pewresearch.org/social-trends/2022/06/28/americans-complex-views-on-gender-identity-and-transgender-issues/

[12] U.S Department of Health and Human Services Office for Civil Rights (2022) HHS notice and guidance on gender affirming care, civil rights, and patient privacy.

[13] Funakoshi and Raychaudchuri (2023).

[14] Shehzad et al (2017).

Key resources

American Civil Liberties Union (ACLU) (2023) Mapping attacks on LGBTQ rights in U.S. state legislatures. Available from: https://www.aclu.org/legislative-attacks-on-lgbtq-rights?impact=health.

Boerner, H. (2022) What the science on gender-affirming care for transgender kids really shows: laws that ban gender-affirming treatment ignore the wealth of research demonstrating its benefits for trans people's health. *Scientific American*. Available from: https://www.scientificamerican.com/article/what-the-science-on-gender-affirming-care-for-transgender-kids-really-shows/

Funakoshi, M. and Raychaudchuri, D. (2023) The rise of anti-trans bills in the U.S. *Reuters*. Available from: https://www.reuters.com/graphics/USA-HEALTHCARE/TRANS-BILLS/zgvorreyapd/

MacDonald, V., Verster, A., Mello, M. B., Blondeel, K., Amin, A., Luhmann, N et al (2022) The World Health Organization's work and recommendations for improving the health of trans and gender diverse people. *Journal of International AIDS Society*, 25(S5): e26004.

McNamara, M., Abdul-Latif, H., Boulware, S. D., Kamody, R., Kuper, L. E., Olezeski, C. L., et al (2023) Combating scientific disinformation on gender affirming care. *Pediatrics*: e2022060943.

Nadeem, S., LaVoi, N., Cooky, C., Buzivis, E., and Staurowsky E. J. (2017) Title IX at XLV. *Contexts: Sociology for the Public* 16(3): 10–19.

Rafferty, J., Committee on Psychosocial Aspects of Child and Family Health, Committee on Adolescence, Section on Lesbian, Gay, Bisexual, and Transgender Health and Wellness, Yogman, M., Baum, R. et al (2018) Ensuring comprehensive care and support for transgender and gender non-conforming children and adolescents. *Pediatrics*, 142(4): e20182162.

Redfield, E., Conron, K. J., Tentido, W., and Browning, E. (2023) Prohibiting gender-affirming medical care for youth. The Williams Institute, UCLA: Los Angeles, CA. Available from: https://williamsinstit ute.law.ucla.edu/wp-content/uploads/Trans-Youth-Health-Bans-Mar-2023.pdf

Shuster, S. M. and Westbrook, L. (2022) Reducing the joy deficit in sociology: a study of transgender joy. Social Problems: spac034. Available from: https://doi.org/10.1093/socpro/spac034

Tordoff, D. M., Wanta, J. W., Collin, A. (2022) Mental health outcomes in transgender and nonbinary youths receiving gender-affirming care. *JAMA Network Open* 5(2): e220978.

THIRTEEN

At the nexus of reproductive and juvenile (in)justice: the (re)production of sexual and reproductive health disparities for system-impacted Black girls

Raquel E. Rose and McKenzie Berezin

The problem

Criminal legal systems are some of the largest providers of physical and mental health care in the United States yet scholars, health professionals, and system-impacted individuals have continuously pointed out the lack of dignified, client-centered sexual and reproductive health (SRH) care received within these settings. The juvenile legal system (also referred to as the juvenile justice system)[1] is tasked with providing those services for young people ages 12–18 when in the custody of the state. A 2006 study by Gallagher and Dobrin found that, while juvenile detention centers partially meet some of the minimum standards for the provision of healthcare services suggested by the National Commission on Correctional Health Care (2004), services were only provided on an ad hoc basis and, for some portions of the population rather than systematic access for all individuals within this system. The study also found geographic and racial differences in quality and scope of services for those in the legal system. Lastly, while there are mandates that require access to SRH care in correctional settings, these mandates do not apply to the significant number of youth who are under the gaze of a punitive system but supervised in the community, therefore leaving many youth underserved.

Discrepancies in quality SRH care for adolescents in the juvenile legal system are especially alarming when examining the paucity of effective SRH care services for a particularly invisibilized and underserved group in the juvenile legal system: system impacted Black girls ages 12–18. The past 20 years have seen lower relative decreases in girls' rates of arrests for a variety of offenses, including status offenses and violent crimes. However, Black girls are far more likely than their White counterparts to have juvenile legal system contact in childhood and adolescence. Black girls are disproportionately disciplined for subjective behaviors such as being disruptive, "incorrigible" and defiant. They are also subjected to more severe punishments for similar offenses, continue to receive differential treatment throughout their trajectory in the juvenile legal system, and are perceived by juvenile legal staff as more manipulative and prone to lying.[2] Also, the reasons for girls' disruptive behavior problems are unique compared to boys'. Structural inequality that creates and perpetuates urban poverty confers greater risk for gendered violence, particularly childhood sexual abuse and trauma, among girls of color. Legally-involved Black girls, whether prior to or during legal contact, also face significant health risks (higher STD/ STI exposure) and unmet health needs across a range of critical resources (reproductive, dental, and mental health) at higher rates than their White female and male peers. These risks are compounded by sociopolitical dynamics where Black girls are simultaneously stigmatized, treated as more mature than they developmentally are (adultified), yet have overall less autonomy than their peers. Additionally, despite reporting an overall higher need for care, Black teen mothers impacted by the juvenile and child welfare systems face the likelihood of additional legal violations *because* of gendered and racial perceptions that Black mothers are inadequate in comparison to their White peers. This leaves Black teen mothers with fewer chances or resources to parent their children with dignity and in safety.

Research evidence

Inherent in the treatment of women and girls seeking reproductive care is an assumption that they are unable to make informed, beneficial decisions regarding the care of them and their children. This sexist and paternalistic ideology not only creates restrictive programming and policy for those most in need of these services, but actively undermines their health and well-being. We see these beliefs interwoven into current SRH care in the United States which has been built on a bedrock of obstetric violence and racism. For example, history underscores the inequitable value placed on Black women's SRH when we consider that many of the "discoveries" of the "father of gynecology," J. Marion Sims, were unethical experiments conducted on Black women.[3] Still today, Black mothers are far less likely to receive prenatal care and are more likely to experience complications during labor and delivery, including providers' disregard of their reported symptoms and higher rates of maternal mortality.[4] Even more recently, with the overturning of *Roe v. Wade*, marginalized girls and women continue to face a unique confluence of sociopolitical factors that strip them of rights, humanity, and agency when attempting to make SRH choices and access SRH services. Black girls in particular face high rates of interpersonal and SRH violence, from dating violence to child sexual trafficking. Additionally, among system-impacted girls of color, anywhere from 20–50 percent of Black and Latinx girls' contract STIs, and unintended pregnancy (UIP) rates range from 25–29 percent among detained girls of color.[5,6] Rather than offering empathic and comprehensive community-based services to address girls' needs, legal stakeholders (police, judges, and so on) stigmatize girls and believe that they are solely responsible for these experiences. Consequently, Black girls receive differential treatment focused on punishment rather than being connected to supportive intervention. Additionally, research efforts to learn more about ways to improve SRH care access and utilization have focused more on disease prevalence and mortality rather than prevention.

Further marginalization happens for legal-involved Black teen mothers under the guise of "protection of children". Historically, the denigration of Black motherhood in the Unites States has been tied to stereotypes of "female promiscuity" and "absentee Black fathers" which led to popular beliefs about "welfare mothers" who were neglectful of their children and only sought to collect government benefits for financial gain. These beliefs contributed to increased scrutiny of the Black family and more opportunities to deem Black mothers as unfit. Cultural beliefs have guided social policies and practices that curtail their sexual and reproductive rights. Legal involved Black teen mothers are especially vulnerable as they bear the weight of this scrutiny but are not equipped developmentally to do so. As such these mothers may run foul of the law and can be simultaneously excessively punished, not only driving both legal involvement and sexual and reproductive vulnerability for Black girls (for example, trafficking and the Commercial Sexual Exploitation of Children (CSEC), domestic abuse), but also puts young moms' infants at risk for foster care involvement. Foster care involvement can have longer-term, intergenerational impact as young mothers miss critical bonding time needed for proper infant development.

Additionally, the overturning of *Roe v. Wade* has permanently skewed the landscape of SRH, with the most vulnerable unsure of the future of their sexual and reproductive rights. *Roe v. Wade* only provided a baseline legal protection; therefore, access to abortion services was still influenced by individuals' state of residence and prevalent ideology in the area. When the Supreme Court reversed this protection, nine states immediately banned this vital SRH right via "trigger laws," designed to take effect once *Roe V. Wade* was no longer applicable.[7] Currently, the outlook is even bleaker with 22 states banning or restricting access to abortion services. There has been a cascade of subsequent conservative-leaning laws that further impede accessibility to care which is exacerbated by race and class. Women who currently live in restrictive states may consider traveling to states with more supportive policy and SRH practices, a decision which requires both emotional and financial resources, or settle with the fewer options in their environment. While the current state of abortion access does not constitute the entirety of the conversation around SRH, it is a key benchmark and serves as a pivotal call-to-action for many who are involved in the effort to improve SRH services.

Recommendations and solutions

To address the ongoing reproductive health injustices that systems-impacted Black girls experience, we promote youth-led, gender- and trauma-responsive changes that simultaneously increase access to quality and safe SRH care and dispel the myth that Black, system-impacted girls cannot be informed participants in their own SRH care.

Leveraging research as a tool for reproductive justice advocacy

- There is a need to prioritize research that centers the voices and perspectives of system-impacted Black girls to meaningfully disrupt the stigmatizing experiences and inaccessibility to care that are telltale characteristics of reproductive injustice. This includes:
  - Leveraging underutilized methodologies—such as qualitative, mixed-method, and participatory research designs—that can more effectively document the complex interpersonal and structural disparities system-impacted Black girls experience in seeking effective and quality SRH care. These methods explicitly center the opinions and experiences of the individuals most affected by the issue.
  - Creating research questions that build a better understanding of how system-impacted Black girls' social locations influence their ability to access equitable and safe SRH care, including their racial and ethnic identities, socioeconomic class, age, and sexual orientation.
  - Ensuring that research promotes evidence-based care and facilitates partnership across systems of care to promote safer, more accessible, and better quality SRH care for system-impacted Black girls.

Programmatic solutions: gender- and trauma-responsive physical and behavioral health services

- Existing research finds that SRH practices that explicitly attend to girls' gender and racial identities and trauma experiences are critical for ensuring reproductive justice for system-impacted Black girls. Trauma- and gender-responsive practices found to be most effective include:
  - Providers' explicit attention to the ways that trauma experiences confer health risk for girls, for example, focusing on risk resulting from abuse

or other forms of gender-based violence, rather than scrutinizing or punishing girls for their SRH risk. This can include, for example:

- Systematically assessing how various experiences of trauma or violence contribute to system-impacted girls presenting SRH needs.
- Providing compassionate care that reduces stigma or shame about system-impacted girls' SRH vulnerabilities. Examples of this care can include trauma-informed language (for example, prohibiting the use of the term "prostitute" when referring to girls experiencing sexual exploitation), the provision of a personalized SRH hygiene bag, or accompaniment by advocate to attend difficult medical appointments.[8]

- Providing collaborative care that prioritizes girls' agency and decision-making; for example, assessing what girls' personal SRH goals are and providing treatment that aligns with their goals rather than providers' goals.
- Cultivating a relationship between providers and youth; for example, ensuring girls see the same provider consistently across their care or ensuring providers take the time to learn about who girls are beyond their SRH needs.
- Identifying and reducing barriers to increase access to quality care (for example, limited availability of providers/sites for accessing services, language barriers, lack of access to electronic medical records, and so on).
- Gender- and trauma-responsive care can and should also be implemented within settings that provide care to system-impacted girls of color. For example:
  - Ensuring systematic training for all healthcare staff on the experiences of system-impacted Black girls that includes:
    - Knowledge of broader contexts and experiences that increase girls' SRH vulnerability such as experiences of gender-based violence or involvement in legal and child welfare systems.
    - How to provide gender- and trauma-responsive services, such as those just described, when working individually with girls.
  - Providing trauma screening for all young people receiving care within healthcare facilities, child welfare, and/or juvenile legal system settings.
  - Modifying organizational policies to ensure the safety and agency of system-impacted Black girls, particularly regarding SRH care. For example:
    - Modifying policies that allow for the use of physical restraint and, instead, requiring restorative justice practices particularly for girls who are within a confined or inpatient setting. Policy modification is particularly important given the evidence that finds how restraints exacerbate trauma symptoms associated with experiences of gender-based violence.

- Ensuring free and easy access to SRH resources for system-impacted girls, such as availability of tampons in facility bathrooms and access to preferred birth control methods.
- Expand the mandate of access to SRH services for legally-involved girls to those who are living outside of correctional facilities in order to account for the needs of Black girls who are under supervision in the community.
- We also recommend increased collaboration between legal, health care, and academic institutions to examine the consistent implementation of effective health care for all youth, particularly SRH care services, while in the custody of child welfare and legal systems. Indeed, while the National Commission on Correctional Health Care has established guidelines to ensure that quality of care is maintained across legal facilities, the creation and delivery of such services varies significantly across sites. Specifically, a collaboration among multidisciplinary scholars (such as experts in child development, reproductive health, implementation scientists), youth themselves, and child welfare or legal system institutions could better ensure that:
  - Quality gender- and trauma-responsive services are delivered to Black girls in child welfare and/or juvenile legal settings.
  - Barriers that impact Black girls' ability to access SRH care and resources are reduced while under the custody of child welfare or juvenile legal system.

Law and policy

- We also recommend increased public and private insurance coverage of all SRH services for youth, and an expanded network of SRH service providers who accept varied types of insurance. While Medicaid is an option for insurance coverage for many, there is a drastic shortage of service providers in some regions, and not all providers accept Medicaid; this is a key limiter of accessibility. This barrier is particularly evident in areas that already experience a "desert" of general health care services.
- Related to the point discussed previously, we also recommend bolstering the existing incentive programs for medical and mental health professionals (particularly those trained in obstetrics and mental health services) to select underserved sites for training and career opportunities such as the American Psychological association fellowship programs, the National Institute of Health Loan Repayment Program, and state supported loan repayment programs.
- While certain areas offer free or low-cost SRH, counseling, and legal services without the requirement of parental permission for youth as young as 12 years old, this is not the case throughout the country. Access to—and confidentiality around—basic SRH needs to be provided nation-wide.

- We recommend incentivizing juvenile legal/child welfare organizations to protect the parent–child dyad through supportive services and community-based placements. Indeed, youth participatory action research (YPAR) finds that both Black girls receiving services and staff working with girls and their families believe that there is a lack of parenting support for system-impacted girls, a lack of supportive placement with their children in the community, and a fear of young parents being separated from their child due to the preference to adopt babies and toddlers over teenagers.
- We also strongly recommend repealing any laws that criminalize people seeking abortions, doctors who perform abortions, organizations that provide follow-up services following negative pregnancy outcomes like stillbirths and miscarriage, and mothers who use drugs during pregnancy.

Notes

[1] We use the terms Criminal legal system and Juvenile legal system, rather than "Justice system" to describe the current recognition by both scholars and activists that these systems have been influenced by previous inequitable structures (slavery and Jim Crow policies) and continue to reinforce inequities rather than providing underserved communities with protection and justice.

[2] Gaarder, E., Rodriguez, N., and Zatz, M. S. (2017) Criers, liars, and manipulators: probation officers' views of girls. In M. Chesney-Lind and M. Morash (Eds) *Feminist Theories of Crime*. Routledge, 345–76.

[3] Owens, D. C. (2017) *Medical Bondage: Race, Gender, and the Origins of American Gynecology*. University of Georgia Press.

[4] Glazer, K. B. and Howell, E. A. (2021) A way forward in the maternal mortality crisis: addressing maternal health disparities and mental health. *Archives of Women's Mental Health*, 24(5): 823–30.

[5] Acoca, L. (2004) Are those cookies for me or my baby? Understanding detained and incarcerated teen mothers their children. *Juvenile and Family Court Journal*, 55(2): 65–80.

[6] Gray, S. C., Holmes, K., and Bradford, D. R. (2016) Factors associated with pregnancy among incarcerated African American adolescent girls. *Journal of Urban Health*, 93(4): 709–18.

[7] Patel, N. (2022) Abortion "trigger" ban statutes: impacts on Plan B, birth control, and IVF treatments. *Georgetown Journal of Gender and the Law*, 73: 1–4.

[8] https://youthlaw.org/news/ca-law-affirms-there-no-such-thing-child-prostitute

Key resources

Berezin, M. N., Javdani, S., and Godfrey, E. (2022) Predictors of sexual and reproductive health among girls involved in the juvenile legal system: the influence of resources, race, and ethnicity. *Children and Youth Services Review*, 136: 106426.

Gallagher, C. A. and Dobrin, A. (2007) Can juvenile justice detention facilities meet the call of the American Academy of Pediatrics and National Commission on Correctional Health Care? A national analysis of current practices. *Pediatrics*, 119(4): e991–e1001.

Hayes, C. M., Sufrin, C., and Perritt, J. B. (2020) Reproductive justice disrupted: Mass incarceration as a driver of reproductive oppression. *American Journal of Public Health*, 110(S1): S21–S24.

Ketteringham, E. S., Cremer, S., and Becker, C. (2016) Healthy mothers, healthy babies: a reproductive justice response to the "womb-to-foster-care pipeline". *CUNY Law Review*, 20: 77.

National Commission on Correctional Health Care (2004) *Standards for Health Services in Juvenile Detention and Confinement Facilities*. National Commission on Correctional Health Care.

Rose, R.E. and Javdani, S. (2023 Gendered surveillance: a critical analysis of legal system actors' attributions of girls' behaviors. In B. Russell and C. Torres (eds) *Perceptions of Female Offenders*. Vol. 1, Springer. https://doi.org/10.1007/978-3-031-42007-8_2

Rosenthal, L. and Lobel, M. (2020) Gendered racism and the sexual and reproductive health of Black and Latina Women. *Ethnicity & Health*, 25(3): 367–92.

Tam, C. C., Dauria, E. F., Cook, M. C., Ti, A., Comfort, M., and Tolou-Shams, M. (2019) Justice involvement and girls' sexual health: directions for policy and practice. *Children and Youth Services Review*, 98: 278–83.

Wennerstrom, A., Sugarman, M., Martin, D., Lobre, C. B., Haywood, C. G., and Niyogi, A. (2022) "You have to be almost dead before they ever really work on you in prison": A qualitative study of formerly incarcerated women's health care experiences during incarceration in Louisiana, US. *Health & Social Care in the Community*, 30(5): 1763–74.

Young Womens' Freedom Center (2022) *When Young Mothers Thrive*. Available from: https://youngwomenfree.org/research/when-young-moth ers-thrive/#:~:text=This%20report%20is%20dedicated%20to,their%20ha rdships%20and%20beautiful%20experiences.

FOURTEEN

Centering racial justice in the US emergency response framework

Sophie Webb

The problem

The United States emergency response framework is crucial for safeguarding public safety and well-being during times of crises, be it natural disasters or public health emergencies. Nevertheless, racial inequities persistently undermine the efficacy of the US federal emergency response system as communities of color shoulder an undue share of the emergency burden, confronting heightened vulnerability, restricted access to resources, and deficient support systems. The heart of the issue lies in the failure of the US emergency response framework to adequately address and rectify systemic disparities, perpetuating historic and ongoing social, economic, and environmental racism. This inability to grapple with pre-existing inequities privileges Whites and further marginalizes racial and ethnic minorities during times of crisis.

Left unaddressed, systemic racial inequalities in resource allocation, relief efforts, and decision-making processes heighten the vulnerability of communities of color, imposing a disproportionate burden during emergencies. Seminal moments, like Hurricane Katrina, became catalysts for public health responders to recognize and address racial disparities in emergency response. More recent instances, including Hurricane Harvey as well as the H1N1 and COVID-19 pandemics, underscore the persistent challenges faced by marginalized communities, revealing ongoing disparities in mortality rates and access to life-saving resources.

Furthermore, two significant strategies of the US emergency response framework reproduce racial inequalities during disasters—data-driven decision-making and utilitarianism. Decision-makers often analyze large datasets and rely on statistical models to identify areas of need, allocate resources, and prioritize interventions. Data-driven decision-making is seen as an objective and efficient method that allows for evidence-based choices. The assumption is that by incorporating various social variables—including race—into algorithms and tools like the Social Vulnerability Index, decision-makers can account for social inequities and tailor responses to meet the specific needs of different communities. However, data-driven approaches tend to prioritize measurable and quantifiable factors, which may overlook more nuanced or qualitative aspects of social inequities. Additionally, data-driven decision-making does not fully address the underlying social determinants that contribute to racial disparities. Even if the data identifies areas with high vulnerability, it may not account for the root causes of these vulnerabilities, such as unequal access to healthcare, education, or economic opportunities.

Additionally, emergency response in the US tends to employ a utilitarian ethic which aims to maximize overall welfare and minimize harm to the greatest number of people. The utilitarian focus on the majority population can overlook the unique challenges faced by vulnerable and historically disadvantaged groups during crises. This approach also tends to prioritize immediate and visible needs, often neglecting the long-term impacts on marginalized communities. Resource allocation and recovery efforts may be directed toward areas with the highest concentration of population, overlooking smaller, marginalized communities that are equally in need but lack visibility and political clout. Consequently, these underserved communities face prolonged recovery periods and greater challenges in rebuilding and restoring their lives after a crisis.

Research evidence

Racial disparities in emergency response

In times of emergencies, communities of color face increased vulnerability and restricted access to essential resources and support systems compared to White communities. Racial inequities in emergency response are further perpetuated by disparities in resource allocation, relief efforts, and decision-making processes. Hurricanes Katrina in 2005 and Harvey in 2017 are poignant examples of the inadequate attention given to pre-crisis conditions by US emergency response policy makers that then exacerbate disparities in crisis outcomes and post-crisis responses. During Hurricane Katrina, predominantly Black communities in New Orleans faced difficulties evacuating due to a lack of reliable transportation options and insufficient disaster notification systems. Historical discrimination, including redlining and racial segregation of neighborhoods, means poor communities of color often live closer to floodplains in areas with aging infrastructure. In the aftermath of the storm, these communities struggled to rebuild as areas with higher property values received substantially more disaster recovery payments, exacerbating challenges for low-income areas—as of 2016, only 60 percent of the historic Black neighborhood of the Seventh Ward had been rebuilt. Likewise, after Hurricane Harvey in 2017, survivors were less likely to receive Federal Emergency Management Agency (FEMA) recovery grants if they resided in a non-White neighborhood and FEMA's recovery funding programs are often only available for homeowners, disproportionately impacting Black and Latinx people who are more likely to rent than their White counterparts.

These inequities extend beyond natural disasters, as evident in the two most recent pandemics. During the 2009 H1N1 pandemic, non-White patients experienced faster deterioration, slower recovery, and higher mortality rates compared to their White counterparts. Researchers found limited access to sick leave for non-White workers and poor housing conditions, marked by overcrowding, hindered their ability to self-quarantine. These factors contributed significantly to health disparities, emphasizing the impact of pre-existing inequalities on the disparities seen during a pandemic. In 2020, communities of color once again suffered higher infection and mortality rates during the COVID-19 pandemic and these communities again faced challenges accessing adequate healthcare and public health services. Barriers such as lack of internet access to book a vaccination appointment, time constraints for appointment booking, transportation difficulties, and the location of most vaccine sites far from communities of color, resulted in Black and Latinx people being vaccinated at rates significantly lower than their share of state populations. In response, FEMA launched the Vaccination Center Pilot Program in 2021 aimed at supplementing state and jurisdictional vaccination efforts. The program was explicitly designed to provide vaccines to racialized groups and demonstrates an effort by the federal emergency response system to reach underserved communities, but the outcomes reveal concerning disparities. Despite targeting populations most in need, Black and Latinx people received fewer doses relative to their population shares in counties with these vaccination centers indicating vaccine distribution disparities persisted despite FEMA's explicit efforts to allocate the vaccine equitably. FEMA's own data illustrate these disparities, per a Government Accountability Office report staff at one such vaccination center noted the majority of those vaccinated in the initial days of operation were White, not the intended Black population. In response, FEMA adapted their strategy by adjusting hours of operation and appointment requirements to prioritize the local Black community, but the question remains why FEMA did not initially operate these sites with extended hours considering time constraints are a well-known barrier to accessing vaccines.

The role of data-driven approaches perpetuating racial disparities

Data-driven approaches, such as the Social Vulnerability Index (SVI), play a crucial role in identifying areas of vulnerability during emergencies. Developed by the CDC in response to the Pandemic and All-Hazards Preparedness Act of 2006, the SVI attempts to account for various social factors that can influence a community's ability to prepare for, respond to, and recover from a crisis, including socioeconomic status, housing conditions, access to transportation, language barriers, and minority status. By analyzing these social factors, the SVI creates an index that ranks communities based on their relative vulnerability, with higher scores indicating greater vulnerability. The SVI is a key resource for the CDC and FEMA, and is used by virtually every state public health department in the US.

However, the SVI does not delve into the deep-rooted social, economic, and political factors that perpetuate racial inequalities and make communities of color more vulnerable to disasters. For example, although a high unemployment rate increases a community's vulnerability, the SVI has been known to rank a community as "less vulnerable" even as its unemployment rate rises.[1] Consequently, relying solely on the SVI or similar data-driven tools might overlook the larger structural issues that contribute to racial disparities in emergency outcomes and could result in marginalized communities being insufficiently prioritized. Case in point, FEMA placed its mass vaccination sites in counties with higher SVIs, but these centers fell short of their intended goal to close the vaccine disparity gap, illustrating that simply applying the SVI to a given area is not enough to understand why it is vulnerable. Similarly, a study assessing the accuracy of the SVI using data from Hurricane Sandy revealed that the SVI did not accurately predict the social vulnerability of the affected areas. For example, Manhattan was classified as highly vulnerable by the SVI because of the large number of renters and people without cars.[2] However, in Manhattan, these factors indicate a densely developed, expensive downtown area with high reliance on public transportation rather than high social vulnerability.

Recommendations and solutions

Rectifying the entrenched racial disparities in the US emergency response framework requires policy makers adopt a comprehensive approach that prioritizes social justice and racial equity in every facet of emergency planning and response. Specifically, federal agencies such as the CDC and FEMA need to commit to centering equity in their data tools and resource allocation guidelines. However, the implementation of these solutions is likely more practical at the state and local levels. State and local health departments, along with disaster response officials, are better positioned to collaborate directly with the communities they serve, ensuring that emergency responses are fair, just, and inclusive.

Data collection and analysis: advancing equity-centered approaches

To effectively address racial disparities in emergency response, it is imperative that policy makers use equity-centered data collection and analysis methods, ensuring they capture the complexity of social inequities and avoid reductionist approaches. Improved data infrastructure and thoughtful analysis will help policy makers identify areas in need of targeted support during emergencies, monitor disparities in real-time, and foster informed decision-making.

- Investment in robust data infrastructure

    To better understand the nuances of social inequities during emergencies, policy makers must invest in data infrastructure that collects and disaggregates information by race, ethnicity, socioeconomic status, and other relevant variables. This approach will allow for a more comprehensive understanding of how different communities experience emergencies and the varying levels of vulnerability they face. Rather than relying solely on pre-existing indices, policy makers should work collaboratively with experts from diverse fields, including social scientists, community advocates, and local stakeholders, to develop meaningful indicators. More holistic alternatives to the SVI include the Canadian Social Vulnerability Model (CanSVM) which uses a hierarchical framework with approximately 20 indicators, measuring absolute disparity and cumulative factors that influence community resilience, including social capital, autonomy, housing, and financial agency. A similarly bespoke American model should consider variable-specific weights based on thorough consultation and research. For example, researchers in Vietnam crafted a new SVI using qualitative interviews with environmental experts and a household survey to gauge locally specific vulnerabilities. In Kenya, researchers tailored the SVI to the local context by conducting focus group discussions with their target population on what they believed made them vulnerable. The goal is to avoid oversimplification and ensure that the indicators accurately capture the unique challenges faced by different communities during emergencies.

- Culturally sensitive and privacy-preserving data collection

    Ethical data collection practices are essential to building trust with marginalized communities and ensuring that their perspectives are adequately represented. Policy makers should collaborate with these communities to design data collection methods that are culturally sensitive and protect individual privacy. This collaborative process will allow for the collection of valuable insights while respecting the rights and interests of those being studied. Before utilizing any data tool or index in public policy, it is crucial to subject it to a robust assessment of its utility. This process should include feedback from community members and experts and ensure that the indicators chosen align with the unique experiences and vulnerabilities of different racial and ethnic groups. Utilizing community-based participatory research methods and ongoing feedback loops can enhance the validity and reliability of the data collected and used.

- Advanced analytical techniques and transparency

    To uncover hidden patterns and potential biases in emergency response efforts, policy makers should use advanced analytical techniques. Instead of relying solely on composite indices, policy makers should consider the potential benefit of communicating variable covariance. Moreover, these techniques must be transparent, and the emphasis should be on an interpretable analysis that facilitates meaningful insights, rather than complex statistical models that obscure the underlying issues. Understanding how different vulnerability factors co-occur in specific geographic areas can inform targeted outreach and preparedness planning across the state. By providing emergency managers with direct links between vulnerability factors and actionable strategies, the decision-making process becomes more informed and responsive to the needs of marginalized communities.

- Continuous evaluation and iterative improvement

     To ensure ongoing improvement in emergency response efforts, policy makers should establish procedures for continuous evaluation. Regularly assessing the outcomes of crisis interventions, with a specific focus on racial and ethnic disparities, will facilitate iterative improvements and evidence-based decision-making. Policy makers must be open to learning from both academic research and real-world emergency response outcomes. Collaborating with researchers and incorporating their findings into policy discussions can lead to more effective and equitable responses. Additionally, policy makers should actively seek feedback from communities affected by emergencies to understand the impact of their policies and make necessary adjustments.

Equitable resource allocation: prioritizing vulnerable communities

Addressing racial disparities in emergency response requires an equity-centered approach to resource allocation. While data-driven tools like the SVI provide valuable insights, as argued, they must be augmented with more comprehensive and nuanced analyses that capture the intricate nature of social inequities. Policy makers should leverage historical as well as qualitative data on community health, access to resources, and socioeconomic indicators to identify areas with heightened vulnerability, thereby enhancing the effectiveness of emergency responses and addressing racial disparities.

- The EEFA Framework

     Inspired by the Canadian Ethics, Equity, Feasibility, Acceptability (EEFA) Framework, US policy makers have an opportunity to develop their own framework for ethical and equitable resource allocation. The EEFA Framework is a peer-reviewed tool that helps public health decision-makers evaluate the ethical, equity, feasibility, and acceptability implications of public health interventions. The Equity aspect of the framework focuses on whether the intervention considers and addresses any existing health disparities or inequities in the target population, thus prioritizing social justice and racial equity in any policy derived from the framework. US policy makers should collaboratively craft a framework that aligns with America's unique historical context and values. Drawing on the EEFA Framework's success in Canada, US policy makers should work in consultation with experts, community advocates, and stakeholders to design a framework that ensures just, equitable, and effective resource allocation during emergencies. By integrating ethics and equity, such a framework could guide decision-makers in addressing racial disparities and promoting fairness in resource distribution.

- Equitable resource allocation

  Developing clear guidelines for distributing critical resources during emergencies, such as vaccines during a pandemic or emergency shelter during a natural disaster, is crucial. The US-tailored EEFA framework's Equity Matrix can serve as the foundation for these guidelines. To populate the Equity Matrix, decision-makers examine the available evidence regarding the impact of various social determinants on potential health inequities in the disaster defined by the acronym P²ROGRESS And Other Factors:

  Place of residence

  Race/ethnicity/culture/language/immigrant or refugee status

  Occupation

  Gender identity/sex

  Religion/belief system

  Education/literacy level

  Socioeconomic status

  Social capital

  Pre-existing conditions

  Age

  Other variables including risk behaviors (smoking, alcohol, and drug use disorder)

- Once decision-makers have considered all the evidence of the impact of P²ROGRESS And Other Factors on a population's vulnerability to a crisis, they conduct research into why the identified health inequities exist (such as differential access to vaccines during a pandemic or the impact of place of residence on proximity to flooding during a hurricane).

  Finally, once decision-makers have identified what health inequities exist during a disaster and how they can impact vulnerability and outcomes, they weave justice into their emergency response and allocation decisions by considering two key questions from prior research: "Is the recommendation equitable in terms of accessibility of the resource for all target groups? Are there special considerations for vulnerability of those most at risk?" By adhering to the EEFA framework's Equity Matrix, policy makers can address systemic marginalization, shaping an allocation strategy that challenges and disrupts racial disparities, rather than perpetuating them.

Pre-disaster planning: fostering inclusivity and empowerment

Perhaps the most important step in ensuring a more racially just and equitable emergency response framework is to include diverse representatives and engage in equity-minded disaster planning well before a crisis emerges. Inclusive disaster planning and community engagement are crucial for developing effective and equitable emergency responses. Policy makers should invest in culturally tailored public education campaigns to disseminate emergency preparedness information to underserved communities.

- Fostering inclusivity and empowerment

    Policy makers must embark on a multi-faceted approach that proactively aims to address the unique needs of marginalized communities. Specifically, policy makers must invest in culturally sensitive public education campaigns that provide information about what to do during a public health crisis and/or natural disaster. These campaigns are vital for breaking down language barriers, navigating literacy differences, and honoring cultural beliefs. Additionally, policy makers need to establish ongoing forums for dialogue between marginalized communities and emergency response decision-makers to uphold transparent and effective collaboration. The goal for these platforms should be to foster trust between government entities, emergency responders, and community representatives.
- Community-led resilience

    A transformative approach to emergency response involves allowing communities to lead disaster preparedness initiatives. Policy makers should forge partnerships with community leaders and organizations to co-create culturally relevant materials and should ensure the representation of diverse racial and ethnic groups within disaster planning committees. This co-creation strategy would leverage the expertise and lived experiences of community leaders to craft solutions that address the unique challenges marginalized communities face before and during a crisis. Through these collaborative approaches, communities become architects of their own safety, resulting in more impactful and effective emergency response strategies.
- Addressing underlying factors

    Finally, policy makers must integrate social factors into pre-disaster planning. Policies that expand access to affordable housing, healthcare, and economic support all increase the resilience of communities and reduce their vulnerabilities, setting the stage for more effective, just emergency responses.

Creating an equitable emergency response system demands a collective and multi-faceted strategy. Through equity-driven data analysis, resource allocation, and community engagement, the US can forge an inclusive framework centered around justice.

Notes

[1] Spielman et al (2020).
[2] Rufat et al (2019).

Key resources

Dembosky, A. (2020) California may consider 'historical injustice' when allocating COVID-19 vaccine. *NPR* [online], December 16. Available from: https://www.npr.org/sections/health-shots/2020/12/16/942452184/california-may-consider-historical-injustice-when-allocating-coronavirus-vaccine

Dorazio, J. (2022) How FEMA can prioritize equity in disaster recovery assistance. Center for American Progress. Available from: https://www.americanprogress.org/article/how-fema-can-prioritize-equity-in-disaster-recovery-assistance/

Flavelle, C. (2021) Why does disaster aid often favor white people? *The New York Times* [online] June 7. Available from: https://www.nytimes.com/2021/06/07/climate/FEMA-race-climate.html

Fussell, S. (2020) The H1N1 crisis predicted Covid-19's toll on Black Americans. *Wired*. Available from: https://www.wired.com/story/h1n1-crisis-predicted-covid-19-toll-black-americans/

Ismail, S. J., Hardy, K., Tunis, M. C., Young, K., Sicard, N., and Quach, C. (2020) A framework for the systematic consideration of ethics, equity, feasibility, and acceptability in vaccine program recommendations. *Vaccine*, 38(36): 5861–76.

Jackson, D. (2021) 500,000 US COVID-19 deaths and counting: a shameful public health failure. *The Equation* (Blog), February 17. Available from: https://blog.ucsusa.org/derrick-jackson/covid-19-deaths-shameful-public-health-failure/

Noguchi, Y. (2021) Race versus time: targeting vaccine to the most vulnerable is no speedy task. *NPR* [online] February 23. Available from: https://www.npr.org/sections/health-shots/2021/02/23/969384904/race-versus-time-targeting-vaccine-to-the-most-vulnerable-is-no-speedy-task

Rufat, S., Tate, E., Emrich, C. T., and Antolini, F. (2019) How valid are social vulnerability models? *Annals of the American Association of Geographers*, 109(4): 1131–53.

Spielman, S. E., Tuccillo, J., Folch, D. C., Schweikert, A., Davies, R., Wood, N., and Tate, E. (2020) Evaluating social vulnerability indicators: criteria and their application to the Social Vulnerability Index. *Natural Hazards*, 100(1): 417–36.

Weller, C. (2023) Climate change worsens natural disasters alongside racial inequality. *Forbes*. Available from: https://www.forbes.com/sites/christianweller/2023/08/17/climate-change-worsens-natural-disasters-alongside-racial-inequality/

PART V

Housing insecurity

Affordable housing in America: a matter of availability, access, and accountability

Jeanne Kimpel

The problem

The idea of the American Dream is consistently connected to homeownership. Research shows that a majority of Americans still see owning a home as one of the most significant measures of success and accomplishment. Yet the average American is unable to afford his or her own home. The lack of affordable housing makes it difficult to buy a home and gain access to a piece of the dream so many wished for growing up. Housing affordability is measured by the share of a person's income spent on a mortgage or monthly rent. Whether a renter or homeowner, if more of one's income is being spent on housing, it means less money for food, transportation, health care, and utilities. Additionally, financial stress brings with it mental stress that can affect one's health. Lack of access to affordable housing is exacerbated by a narrative and culture connected to a legacy of racism and institutional discrimination that has made racial residential segregation a seemingly permanent part of the landscape. Redlining practices, blockbusting, exclusionary zoning policies, and other housing discrimination practices have denied access to housing, neighborhoods, and opportunities that disproportionately affect people of color.[1]

Additional barriers that hinder home purchases include not having enough money for a down payment, wages that do not keep pace with rising housing costs, high mortgage rates, and exclusionary policies. Research on social class, social mobility, and housing clearly shows that homeownership is the primary way that Americans have established financial security and intergenerational wealth. Owning a home typically brings with it many additional benefits, including access to good schools, better resources, economic opportunities, and improved health outcomes. The dearth of affordable housing and the inability of so many people to acquire a sense of well-being, comfort, and financial security contributes to, and exacerbates, other social problems. These include homelessness, poverty, ill health, a racial wealth gap, and reduced educational opportunities.

Research evidence

Research indicates that for several years, millions of families in the US have been impacted by the housing affordability crisis. This problem worsened during the COVID-19 pandemic as inflation, home, and rental prices increased, housing inventory decreased, and incomes largely remained the same. In 2022, the U.S. Department of Housing and Urban Development reported that on any given night, 582,500 people were homeless. Both low-income renters and higher-income families find it challenging to secure housing. In recent years, median prices of houses have fluctuated between $420,000 and $431,000.[2] Towards the end of 2023, The Rent reported that the national median rent is $1,978.[3] This section outlines key factors that contribute to the housing crisis with the aim of proposing viable policy solutions.

- The Pew Research Center reported in 2021 that 85 percent of Americans were concerned about the availability of affordable housing in their local area. Nearly half (49 percent) said it was a major problem, with 70 percent saying that it was a bigger problem now than it was in previous generations.
- According to Freddie Mac, a government-sponsored mortgage corporation, there is a shortage of available housing. Their chief economist estimated that 3.8 million new units would need to be built to help house both renters and buyers.[4]
- Towards the end of 2023, the National Association of Home Builders (NAHB)/Wells Fargo Housing Opportunity Index (HOI), reported only 40.5 percent of new and existing homes sold in the spring were affordable to families with a median income of $96,300.[5] As interest rates for an average 30-year fixed mortgage continued to rise as high as 8 percent, it is clear that even for those with what should considered a great income, owning a home becomes a dream deferred.
- According to The Joint Center for Housing Studies (JCHS) at Harvard University and the American Community Survey (ACS) between 2019 and 2021, there was an increase in the number of households identified as cost burdened and severely burdened respectively. In those 3 years, 40.6 million households spent more than 30 percent of their income on housing, and 20.3 million households spent more than half of their income on housing.[6]
- The renter's market is no better. According to JCHS, in 2021, out of 44 million renter households, almost half of those renters (45 percent) were rent-burdened, meaning that they spent more than 30 percent of their household income on rent.[7]
- Rents for single-family housing reached the fastest rate of increase on record in early 2022, rising 12.4 percent year-over-year in the first quarter. Rents also increased year-over-year in all the nation's large metro markets in early 2022, growing by double digits in 116 out of 150 metro markets.[8]

- Since 2009, the federal minimum wage has remained at $7.25, and while state minimum wages vary, more than half the states in the US have a minimum wage higher than $7.25, but less than $13. With these rates, rising inflation, and the conditions of rent-burdened individuals, it is challenging for those earning such low wages to pay rent every month.
- According to the Bureau of Labor Statistics, median weekly earnings of full-time workers at the end of 2023 were $1,118. When examining median weekly earnings by race and ethnicity, it is clear that there is a racial income gap with Blacks ($918) and Hispanics ($885) earning less compared to Whites ($1,137).[9]
- For those who do own a home, and struggle to pay their monthly mortgage, foreclosure data act as an indicator of the struggles homeowners face making their mortgage payments. According to ATTOM, a leading provider of nationwide property data, the number of foreclosure filings in 2022 (324,237) was reported to have increased 115 percent since 2021. These increases are likely due to the end of COVID-19 moratorium-related protections.[10]
- The lack of affordable units affects the poorest renters the most. In 2021, a report to Congress (2021) on worst-case housing needs explains people in this category (7.7 million), are very low-income renters who do not receive government housing assistance, have incomes at or below 50 percent of the median income, and spend more than 50 percent of their income on rent.[11]
- According to the JCHS and ACS, between 2015 and 2019, 71.7 percent of White households owned their homes in the US compared to 47 percent of households of color. This racial homeownership gap contributes to the racial wealth gap indicating that the average White household has 8 times the wealth of the average Black household.[12]

Recommendations and solutions

Addressing the housing crisis is not a one-dimensional solution. There are multiple issues that influence access to affordable housing. Strategies to mitigate the housing affordability problem need to occur at the federal, state, and local levels using an equitable lens to meet the varied needs of the population. Policy makers, researchers, and officials should work in a productive way to combat the issues outlined in this chapter. First, the US needs to provide more affordable housing; and secondly, the policy makers, academics, non-profits, housing advocates, and local community organizations working on the affordable housing problem, need to improve or change existing policies. They must also seek out and embrace new alternatives.

- According to HUD, the Housing Choice Voucher (HCV) program, also known as Section 8 or Tenant-Based Rental Assistance (TBRA) currently extends help to a little over 2.3 million families in the US. It is the biggest effort by the Federal Government to assist extremely low-income families, people with disabilities, and the elderly, who are listed in the worst-case housing needs report.[13] There is a continued need to increase funding in these areas especially as inflation continues to rise. HUD has introduced a new pilot housing mobility program that offers families with children access to lower poverty neighborhoods and better areas of opportunity. Currently, those receiving housing vouchers must use them in the jurisdiction of the area in which they have lived. This new program would allow a family to move to other neighborhoods or even states, which could provide a better quality of life.[14]
- States and localities should take advantage of a new $85 million Pathways to Removing Obstacles (PRO) housing program promoted by HUD, which will offer up to $10 million in competitive grants to help address housing affordability in their respective areas.[15] The potential to apply funding for rezoning multi-family, mixed-use housing or reducing land-use restrictions is a progressive step toward housing affordability assistance. This program needs to be renewed annually with increased funding across areas.
- People should be encouraged to support alternative programs, ideas, and organizations at the "grassroots" level that could sustain efforts to build and maintain affordable housing units. One such example includes Community Land Trusts (CLTs) as a path to affordable housing. The goal of the CLT is to have groups of people buy land as part of a shared-equity homeownership, and give access to low-income residents of the house—not the land—for long-term tenure. This innovative idea was implemented across 46 states including the District of Columbia. The program has yielded 165 CLTs and almost 12,000 homes.[16]
- An alternative idea introduced on The Housing Solutions Lab website is a new funding opportunity from the Robert Wood Johnson Foundation. A request for proposals encourages members of local government to work in teams to design initiatives aimed at assisting small and midsize cities whose residential numbers fall between 50,000 and 500,000. Some suggestions include opportunities to reduce homelessness, improve housing quality, and those that address zoning or land use.[17]
- A recent bill introduced to the Senate would amend the Fair Housing Act to prohibit discrimination based on source of income, veteran, or military status. The Fair Housing Improvement Act of 2022 would allow

income to include those receiving housing vouchers or other rental assistance.[18] Encourage Congress to pass this bill. It provides protection to people who have been stigmatized or excluded due to their status as an HCV recipient.

- While certain states have raised their minimum wages, there has not been any move on the federal level in over a decade. Rents and housing costs have been steadily rising faster than incomes. Currently, the Raise the Wage Act of 2023 is before Congress and would gradually raise the minimum wage to $15 per hour by 2025.[19] It is recommended that the Federal minimum wage be assessed more frequently to align with inflation.

- Homeowners benefit from many tax deductions, but the same cannot be said for renters. Thirty US economists sent a letter in 2023 to the Federal Housing Finance Agency (FHFA).[20] They appealed to the FHFA to consider federal rental protections amid significant rent increases.

- Another recommendation towards new protections for renters includes a combined effort to improve the Low-Income Housing Tax Credit (LIHTC) along with a federal renters' tax credit.[21]

- Provide continued support and increased funding for the National Housing Trust Fund (NHTF). The National Low Income Housing Coalition (NLICS) has supported this fund that recently provided $693 million dollars to preserve housing for those in low-income households.[22]

- Another innovative idea consists of non-profit groups who formed ROC USA, which provides affordable housing by transforming mobile home parks into resident-owned communities. Part of their role is to provide financial and educational resources for lower-income people.[23]

- In an effort to reduce housing costs, state and local officials should work together to reform zoning laws and land-use controls that have historically excluded people by class and race. Governor Hochul of NY has suggested solutions to the housing shortage issue includes zoning reform. Many of her efforts were met with those chanting "Not in My Backyard" otherwise known as NIMBY supporters. One solution here is to launch educational awareness campaigns to dispel the negative narrative connected to zoning changes. This requires a cultural change in the mindset of lawmakers, policy makers, and constituents alike to have an informative dialogue to reassess the way they perceive zoning reform.

- Accessibility must be increased to education, training, and knowledge for all kinds of housing assistance for renters, current homeowners, and those seeking to purchase a home. Too often people are unaware of the benefits, deductions, programs, subsidies, and policies that could assist them with obtaining affordable housing. When navigating websites, much of the information is only provided in English. It would benefit many others to offer information in multiple languages.

Notes

[1] Rothstein (2017). Rothstein provides clear and supportive evidence that the U.S. government at all levels promoted and created policies, which endorsed racial segregation.

[2] U.S. Census Bureau and U.S. Department of Housing and Urban Development. (2023). *Median Sales Price of Houses Sold for the United States [MSPUS]*. FRED. Available from: https://fred.stlouisfed.org/series/MSPUS

[3] Leckie, J. (2023). *The Rent Report*. Available from: https://www.rent.com/research/average-rent-price-report/

[4] The Economic and Housing Research Group (2021) *Housings Supply: A Growing Deficit*. Freddie Mac. Available from: https://www.freddiemac.com/research/insight/20210507-housing-supply

[5] National Association of Home Builders. (2023) Rising mortgage rates and home prices put a damper on housing affordability. NAHB. Available from: https://www.nahb.org/news-and-economics/press-releases/2023/08/rising-mortgage-rates-and-home-prices-put-a-damper-on-housing-affordability

[6] Whitney, P. (2023) Number of renters burdened by housing costs reached a record high in 2021. Joint Center for Housing Studies. Available from: https://www.jchs.harvard.edu/blog/number-renters-burdened-housing-costs-reached-record-high-2021. Both the JCHS and ACS sites provide reliable and valuable sources to draw from with recent data. Much of the information provided using these sources come from The State of the Nation's Housing Report 2022 and can be downloaded from the JCHS website.

[7] Whitney (2023), see note 6.

[8] Whitney (2023), see note 6.

[9] Bureau of Labor Statistics. U.S. Department of Labor. (2023) Usual weekly earnings of wage and salary workers [Press release], October 18. Available from: https://www.bls.gov/news.release/pdf/wkyeng.pdf. The BLS site provides access to interactive tools and maps to compare data across states, by jobs, race and ethnicity and other categories.

[10] ATTOM (2023) U.S. foreclosure activity doubles annually in 2022 but still below pre-pandemic levels. Available from: https://www.attomdata.com/news/market-trends/foreclosures/attom-year-end-2022-u-s-foreclosure-market-report/

[11] Alvarez and Steffen (2021).

[12] Whitney (2023), see note 6.

[13] Alvarez and Steffen (2021).

[14] Department of Housing and Urban Development. (2022) Section 8 housing choice vouchers: Implementations of the housing choice voucher mobility demonstration for awarded PHAs, supplemental notice for demonstration participants. Federal Register. Available from: https://www.federalregister.gov/documents/2022/04/04/2022-06997/section-8-housing-choice-vouchers-implementation-of-the-housing-choice-voucher-mobility

[15] U.S. Department of Housing and Urban Development. (2023) Pathways to removing obstacles to housing (PRO Housing). HUD.gov. Available from: https://www.hud.gov/program_offices/comm_planning/pro_housing

[16] Thaden and Pickett (2021). See https://groundedsolutions.org for further details on CLTs, inclusionary housing policies, tools and resources.

[17] Local Housing Solutions (2023) Funding Opportunity: Catalyzing housing and health collaborations in small and midsize cities. Available from: https://localhousingsolutions.org/housing-health-funding-opportunity/

[18] Fair Housing Improvement Act of 2022, S4485, 117th Congress (2022) Available from: https://www.congress.gov/bill/117th-congress/senate-bill/4485

19 Raise the Wage Act of 2023, S2488, 118th Congress (2023) Available from: https://www.congress.gov/bill/118th-congress/house-bill/4889/

20 Federal Finance Housing Agency (2023) Tenant protections for enterprise-backed multifamily properties request for input. Available from: https://peoplesaction.org/wp-content/uploads/Economist-Sign-on-Letter_-FHFA-RFI-Response-1.pdf

21 Bailey, P. (2022) Addressing the affordable housing crisis requires expanding rental assistance and adding housing units. Center for Budget and Policy Priorities. Available from: https://www.cbpp.org/research/housing/addressing-the-affordable-housing-crisis-requires-expanding-rental-assistance-and

22 National Low Income Housing Coalition (n.d.). The solution: protect and expand the national housing trust fund. Available from: https://nlihc.org/explore-issues/why-we-care/solution

23 ROC USA. (n.d.). Available from: https://rocusa.org/about-roc-usa/

Key resources

Alvarez, T. and Steffen, B. (2021) *Worst Case Housing Needs 2021 Report to Congress*. U.S. Housing and Urban Development. Available from: https://www.huduser.gov/portal/sites/default/files/pdf/Worst-Case-Housing-Needs-2021.pdf

Dastrup, S., Finkel, M., Burnett, K., and de Sousa, T. (2018) *Small Area Fair Market Rent Demonstration Evaluation: Final Report*. Housing and Urban Development. Available from: https://www.huduser.gov/portal/publications/Small-Area-FMR-Evaluation-Final-Report.html

Fair Housing Improvement Act of 2022, S4485, 117th Congress. (2022) Available from: https://www.congress.gov/bill/117th-congress/senate-bill/4485

Johnson, J. (2023) Renters are struggling: Economists back tenant-led push for federal rent control. Common Dreams. Available from: https://www.commondreams.org/news/economists-rent-control

Joint Studies of Housing for Harvard University (2022) *The State of the Nation's Housing* 2022. Available from: https://www.jchs.harvard.edu/state-nations-housing-2022.

National Low Income Housing Coalition. Raise the Wage Act of 2023, S2488, 118th Congress. (2023) Available from: https://www.congress.gov/bill/118th-congress/house-bill/4889/

Rosen, E. (2020) *The Voucher Promise: "Section 8" and the Fate of an American Neighborhood*. Princeton University Press.

Rothstein, R. (2017) *The Color of Law: A Forgotten History of How Our Government Segregated America*. Liveright.

Thaden, E. and Pickett, T. (2021) Community Land Trusts: combining scale and community control. Shelterforce. Available from: https://shelterforce.org/2021/07/19/community-land-trusts-combining-scale-and-community-control/

SIXTEEN

Shelter from the storm: a framework for housing and climate justice

Tony R. Samara

The Congress hereby declares that the general welfare and security of the Nation and the health and living standards of its people require housing production and related community development sufficient to remedy the serious housing shortage, the elimination of substandard and other inadequate housing through the clearance of slums and blighted areas, and the realization as soon as feasible of the goal of a decent home and a suitable living environment for every American family, thus contributing to the development and redevelopment of communities and to the advancement of the growth, wealth, and security of the Nation.

Housing Act of 1949

We finally cleaned up public housing in New Orleans. We couldn't do it, but God did.

Richard Baker, Louisiana Congressman, 2005[1]

The problem

We did not appreciate it fully at the time, but Hurricane Katrina was a warning to all of us. The storm and its aftermath provided a glimpse into a future where housing insecurity and climate change combine with devastating effect to reshape entire social and physical landscapes. The storm damaged more than a million homes and displaced about a million people. Almost 2,000 residents lost their lives and 3 million required federal assistance in the aftermath.[2] While exact numbers may never be available, we do know that for many the displacement from the city was permanent, and that Black residents, many of them renters or residents of since demolished public housing, were the least likely to return.[3] As of 2020, New Orleans had lost 21 percent of its pre-Katrina population.[4] The response to the storm and the way—and for whom—the city was rebuilt provide a cautionary tale about the intersections of housing, race, and class as we enter a new era of climate change.

Housing insecurity is conventionally measured by affordability, with households paying more than 30 percent of income considered cost burdened. This is a crude and insufficient measure in many ways.[5] It does not, for example, account for overall income—30 percent is clearly not burdensome in any meaningful way for wealthy households, while poor households may be burdened by costs far below the 30 percent threshold. Even by this narrow measure, however, housing insecurity has worsened considerably in recent years for both homeowners and renters. In 2021 almost a third of all households, about 40 million renters and homeowners, experienced housing insecurity. The disparity between renters and homeowners is significant, with 23 percent of homeowners experiencing a cost burden compared with 49 percent of renters.[6]

Climate change must be understood against this backdrop of structural housing precarity. Intense disaster events and long-term changes that make certain places inhabitable are already driving displacement around the world. As always, those most at risk are the most vulnerable and least resourced.[7] In the United States, recent fires, floods and severe temperatures have already caused direct harm to people and are upending housing and housing insurance markets across the county.[8] Climate change also threatens existing affordable housing, makes new construction more difficult, and will push lower income people into more vulnerable areas.[9] If current trends continue, we will see increases in severe heat and cold, water shortages, and mega-fires, all contributing to massive population shifts.[10] The harms are not evenly distributed across regions or populations but it is undeniable that we face a collective threat: many if not most of us need to think about how climate change will affect the places we call home.

For us at the Right to the City Alliance, the arrival of the climate change era is another blow for the low-income and working-class communities of color our members represent. Historically marginalized and segregated, these communities have spent the last 20-plus years resisting gentrification, evictions, and market-driven displacement. Now climate change compounds the challenges we face, adding a new and dangerous dimension to housing security across the country. The challenge before us is to understand how climate, housing, and land are intertwined. From that understanding we must identify effective policies that address short term needs and longer-term transformation to a less extractive, more sustainable world—and we must develop the political power to win and defend these policies.

Research evidence

The years following the Great Recession and the collapse of the housing market brought increased attention to evictions, displacement, and the plight of renters in America more broadly. Tenants and tenant activists in cities across the country had been fighting the gentrification of low-income and working-class communities of color since long before then, but these efforts were often cast as artifacts of a past era in the broad arc of progressive urban "revitalization" beginning in the late 1970s. It was only when the consequences of the financialization of housing came home to roost for homeowners in the 2000s that housing security became a matter of greater public interest and the challenges facing renters for the first time in decades drew national attention.[11]

While the post-recession years saw some relief for homeowners and a rebounding of the for-sale housing market, housing insecurity as measured by rent burden for renters worsened.[12] This period saw an increase in demand, in part because of foreclosures, and a rise in rent-burdened households with very clear racial disparities.[13] The COVID-19 pandemic caused a new round of social and economic disruptions, creating additional hardships for millions of renters.[14] These were partially offset, for a time, by federal action on rents and evictions but as COVID-related assistance and protections sunset the future for working class and low-income renters still looks grim.[15]

Housing insecurity has a range of negative impacts on individuals, families, and communities. Overcrowding, chronic stress related to finances and fear of eviction, multiple moves, poor habitability, loss of social support networks—these are some of the primary manifestations of housing insecurity for millions of renters across the country.[16] Many of these have long term consequences. Research on housing as a social determinant of health, for example, has shown that stressful and unhealthy living conditions interfere with normal childhood development and predispose children to poor health outcomes in adulthood.[17]

Displacement is perhaps the greatest concern from a housing justice perspective because it can degrade the social networks that allow residents to effectively mobilize when emergencies like floods and wildfires occur, and to organize for better living conditions and long-term housing and community security. Research stretching back to the era of urban renewal has shown that displacement disrupts the trajectories of socio-economic development and political power that marginalized communities are able to build despite their marginalization.[18] This is one reason that organizing against evictions has taken on such importance for many tenant activists.

Today, market forces are not the only displacement threat facing housing insecure communities. There is growing awareness of the danger posed by climate change and our lack of preparedness for the impact it will have across the country. A recent survey by Data for Progress found that 47 percent of likely voters fear displacement from a severe weather event and one third had already been displaced or knew someone who had, while only 38 percent believe the federal government provides enough support for disaster relief.[19]

Citing American Housing Survey data, The Joint Center for Housing Studies at Harvard writes that "between 2015-2017 324,000 renters were displaced by natural disasters and more than 500,000 rental units required extensive disaster-related repair."[20] In addition, they estimate that 23 million renter households, or 53 percent of the total, live in urban heat islands, including almost 5 million households making less than $15,000 per year.[21] According the Urban Displacement Project at UC Berkeley,

> there are significant inequities between different socioeconomic and racial groups in vulnerability to the impacts of climate shocks and stressors. Low-income groups and communities of color, particularly African American and Hispanic communities, are often more likely to experience financial hardships related to climate hazards and physical displacement in the wake of extreme weather events. *These inequities play out in varying degrees across every stage of a climate event.* [emphasis added][22]

Despite this and greater economic precarity of renters, federal aid continues to disproportionately favor homeowners over tenants.[23] The result is that climate disasters add to the housing challenges facing many working class and low-income communities, and communities of color in particular.

Recommendations and solutions

The involvement of front-line communities in generating and implementing solutions to the problems they face has a long, and at times controversial history, whether at the scale of international development or local community-organizing.[24] The reasons for centering the residents of impacted communities, however, are many, ranging from their intimate knowledge of local conditions to their deep self-interest in creating meaningful solutions. This at times can put community-based solutions in tension with approaches preferred by elected officials, policy makers, and other experts.[25]

Immense investment into metropolitan real estate markets in recent decades has led to an era of ever-increasing rents, an epidemic of evictions, and a revitalization of tenant organizing across the country over the past 15 years.[26] This period has provided important insights into the challenges under-resourced communities face in addressing short-term threats like evictions and the longer-term goal of household and community health and stability. Importantly, it has allowed organizers, advocates, philanthropy, and allies in policy, law, academia, and government to develop a framework for housing security to address these related challenges. This framework, rooted in the importance of allowing people to remain in their homes and communities, is essential in responding to the emerging threat of climate change.

In the context of organizing for housing security in the United States, centering communities has meant centering the role of renters.[27] The policy solutions framework emerging from the new tenant movement has anti-displacement at its core. The reasoning is fairly straightforward: anti-displacement measures (like rent control and eviction protections) speak to the daily concerns of renter households, especially those with children, whose lives can be permanently harmed by evictions and multiple forced moves.[28] These renter protections can also provide important material benefits to many residents in a relatively short period of time, unlike multi-year plans for small percentages of affordable housing in future construction. Anti-displacement measures also introduce a measure of community stability in addition to stability at the household level. Finally, anti-displacement measures can open up political spaces for residents to consider longer term solutions that protect land and housing from the speculative, for-profit market.

Climate change expands and deepens this framework beyond housing insecurity caused by market forces. Building on the long history of communities of color fighting for environmental justice, newer efforts by housing activists and advocates ground climate and housing justice in the lived realities and political work of front-line communities.[29] A recent effort by my organization, The Right to the City Alliance, seeks to adapt the anti-displacement–decommodification framework to the reality of climate change and its growing impact on front-line communities.[30] The basic framework, many of the relevant policies, and the goals remain the same: allow tenants to live in safe, secure, decent housing. For some issues, climate change exacerbates existing problems and conditions: extreme heat and cold, for example, only increase the need for good insulation and for controlling utility costs, while fires and floods underscore the importance of relocation funds and policies guaranteeing the right to return when that is safe.

Climate change does also introduce the need for new and significantly revised public policies at the local, state, and federal levels over both the near and long term. Disaster recovery, developing household and community resilience to the new climate reality, and building or rebuilding housing in safer areas all represent somewhat new terrain for housing justice. While action at the federal level, covering all states, would be ideal, the political reality is that we are unlikely to see this in the near future. As a result, local and state governments will need to be actively involved in advancing climate and housing justice policies. Here I provide some examples at a variety of scales, drawn from a recent policy platform authored by Kristen Hackett for the Right to the City Alliance.[31]

- Preventing the costs of upgrading or retrofitting buildings for climate-related home improvements from being passed on to tenants and resulting in increased housing costs that can lead to displacement. Example: Pennsylvania Whole Homes Repair Act.[32]
- Ban on resale of disaster-impacted land and housing during and after evacuations coupled with new programs to support sale to public entities

or community-controlled non-profits, similar to the FEMA Flood buy-out program.

- Addressing severe temperatures: weatherization programs targeting low-income renters to ensure all homes are energy efficient, weatherproof, and protected from pollution at low or no cost to residents; right to heat safe housing to provide adequate heating/cooling. Example: the California Weatherization Assistance Program.[33]
- Policies similar to the proposed TREES Act in Oregon, which supports afforestation and views trees as critical public infrastructure.
- Community-controlled renewable energy options, including wind and solar projects to provide energy access and contribute to decarbonization.
- Funding and training for community resilience hubs, which are community centers that centralize and extend community networks. These can be used to address institutional gaps that exclude undocumented residents, serve as centers during and after disasters, and provide spaces for communities to organize and mobilize. These hubs can be connected regionally to extend community networks and expand the reach of community-level aid. Oregon HB2990, for example, would establish a grant program to directly fund communities to build and implement community hubs and networks.[34]
- Train community health workers and other emergency responders using a mutual aid model to support existing services and address gaps left by these.
- Community-based mapping of local and regional geography to account for assess how climate risks are distributed across communities. These efforts can partner with local universities and research centers to support spatial analysis, land surveys, and other technical interventions that will allow communities to engage in longer term planning and climate adaptation.
- Building from this, analysis could also help communities identify land and housing for temporary use during emergencies, for future building, and to plan for managed retreat from areas that may become uninhabitable due to climate change.
- Public land for public good legislation that prevents cities from transferring public land to private developers and prioritizes community land trusts and other forms of community stewardship that align land use with the need for climate adaptation.

Land and housing justice sit at the center of the social, economic, and political transformations that are already underway as a result of climate change and will be central to confronting it. The communities on the front lines of housing and climate crises, by extension, are central subjects in responding to these crises and charting a path forward. The framework outlined here shows what this can look like: protect against displacement, develop resilience to survive the changes already underway, and from this foundation, develop the political momentum to build a less extractive, more sustainable future. While an unprecedented challenge lies in front of us, the converging of housing and climate justice movements represents an exciting and powerful opportunity to make this future real.

Notes

1. Babington, C. (2005) Some GOP legislators hit jarring notes in addressing Katrina, *The Washington Post* [online] September 10. Available from: https://www.washingtonpost.com/wp-dyn/content/article/2005/09/09/AR2005090901930.html

2. Richardson, T. M. (2021) A look back at Katrina, *HUD User*. Available from: https://www.huduser.gov/portal/pdredge/pdr-edge-frm-asst-sec-092121.html

3. Bliss, L. (2015) 10 years later, there's so much we don't know about where Katrina survivors ended up, *Bloomberg* [online] August 25. Available from: https://www.bloomberg.com/news/articles/2015-08-25/8-maps-of-displacement-and-return-in-new-orleans-after-katrina

4. Cornelissen, S. and Jang-Trettien, C. (2023) The sociology of housing: how homes shape our social lives. Joint Center for Housing Studies. Available from: https://www.jchs.harvard.edu/blog/sociology-housing-how-homes-shape-our-social-lives.

5. DeLuca, S. and Rosen, E. (2022) Housing insecurity among the poor today, *Annual Review of Sociology*, 48: 343–71; Stone, M. (1993) *Shelter Poverty: New Ideas on Housing Affordability*, Temple University Press.

6. Habitat for Humanity (2023) *State of the Nation's Housing Report: 4 Key Takeaways for 2023*. Available from: https://www.habitat.org/costofhome/2023-state-nations-housing-report-lack-affordable-housing.

7. Oxfam (2019) *Forced From Home: Climate-Fueled Displacement*, Oxfam Media Briefing, December 2. Available from: https://www.oxfam.org/en/research/forced-home-climate-fuelled-displacement.

8. The Economist (2023) Climate change is coming for America's property market. Available from: https://www.economist.com/leaders/2023/09/21/climate-change-is-coming-for-americas-property-market; Worland, J. (2021) The climate real estate bubble: is the U.S. on the verge of another financial crisis? *Time Magazine* [online] April 19. Available from: https://time.com/5953380/climate-housing-crisis ; Sisson, P. (2020) In many cities, climate change will flood affordable housing, *Bloomberg*, [online] December 1. Available from: https://www.bloomberg.com/news/articles/2020-12-01/how-climate-change-is-targeting-affordable-housing.

9. Fu, S. (2022) How cities can tackle both the affordable housing and climate crises, *Housing Matters*, [online] November 2. Available from: https://housingmatters.urban.org/articles/how-cities-can-tackle-both-affordable-housing-and-climate-crises; Frank, T. (2020) Flooding disproportionately harms black neighborhoods, *Scientific American*, [online] June 2. Available from: https://www.scientificamerican.com/article/flooding-disproportionately-harms-black-neighborhoods/; Wiltz, T. (2019) Climate change is making the affordable housing crunch worse, *Stateline*, [online] August 30. Available from: https://stateline.org/2019/08/30/climate-change-is-making-the-affordable-housing-crunch-worse/.

10. Lustgarten, A. (2020) How climate migration will reshape America, *New York Times* [online] September 15. Available from: https://www.nytimes.com/interactive/2020/09/15/magazine/climate-crisis-migration-america.html.

11. Crump. S. and Schuetz, J. (2021) What the Great Recession can teach us about the post-pandemic housing market, *Brookings Institute*, [online] March 29. Available from: https://www.brookings.edu/articles/what-the-great-recession-can-teach-us-about-the-post-pandemic-housing-market/.

[12] Colburn, G. and Allen, R. (2018) Rent burden and the Great Recession in the USA, *Urban Studies*, 55(1): 226–43.

[13] Pew Research Center (2018) American families face a growing rent burden. Available from: https://www.pewtrusts.org/en/research-and-analysis/reports/2018/04/american-families-face-a-growing-rent-burden; Samara, T. (2014) *Rise of the Renter Nation: Solutions to the Housing Affordability Crisis*, Right to the City Alliance.

[14] Michener, J. and SoRelle, M. (2022) Politics, power, and precarity: how tenant organizations transform local political life. *Interest Groups and Advocacy*, 11: 209–36.

[15] Joint Center for Housing Studies (2022) America's rental housing 2022, Harvard University.

[16] For a useful literature survey, see Housing Instability, *Healthy People 2030*, US Department of Health and Human Services, 2020. Available from: https://health.gov/healthypeople/priority-areas/social-determinants-health/literature-summaries/housing-instability.

[17] San Francisco Department of Public Health (2019) *Health Impacts of Family Housing Insecurity.*

[18] Fullilove, T. M. (2016) *Root Shock: How Tearing Up City Neighborhoods Hurts Americans And What We Can Do About It*, New Village Press.

[19] Israeli, E. (2022) Increasing equitable disaster relief: ending cycles of displacement for low-income renters. *Data for Progress*. Available from: https://www.dataforprogress.org/memos/increasing-equitable-disaster-relief.

[20] Joint Center for Housing Studies (2022), p 37.

[21] Joint Center for Housing Studies (2022), p 38

[22] Cash, A. et al (2020) *Climate Change and Displacement in the U.S. – A Review of the Literature*, Urban Displacement Project, p. 5.

[23] America's Rental Housing (2022), pp 42–3.

[24] Eversole, R. (2012) Remaking participation: challenges for community development practice, *Community Development Journal*, 47(1): 29–41.

[25] Guarneros, V. and Geddes, M. (2010) Local governance and participation under neoliberalism: comparative perspectives, *International Journal of Urban and Regional Research*, 34(1): 115–29.

[26] King, S.R. (2021) Organized tenants are baaack. Shelterforce. Available from: https://shelterforce.org/2022/11/21/organized-tenants-are-back/.

[27] Samara. T. R. (2014) *Rise of the Renter Nation: Solutions to the Housing Affordability Crisis.* Homes for All Campaign of Right to the City Alliance. Available from: https://assets.website-files.com/61ccce7fbdaf706120c7c25f/62ac33d0254d0bc49770123e_RISE-OF-THE-RENTER-NATION_FULL-REPORT_web.pdf

[28] Desmond, M. and Kimbro, R. T. (2015) Eviction's fallout: housing, hardship, and health, *Social Forces*, 94(1): 295–324.

[29] Hackett, K. (2023) *Roots of Resilience & Canopies of Community Stewardship: A Framework For Housing & Climate Justice Policy*, Right to the City Alliance.

[30] The author served as editor for this publication.

[31] Taken from *Roots of Resilience & Canopies of Community Stewardship.*

[32] https://www.legis.state.pa.us/cfdocs/legis/PN/Public/btCheck.cfm?txtType=PDF&sessYr=2021&sessInd=0&billBody=S&billTyp=B&billNbr=1135&pn=1474

[33] https://www.csd.ca.gov/Pages/Residential-Energy-Efficiency.aspx

[34] https://www.orhubs.org/

Key resources

Black Hive (2023) *The Black Climate Mandate*, Movement for Black Lives. Available from: https://m4bl.org/wp-content/uploads/2022/08/The-Black-Climate-Mandate-2022-The-Black-Hive-@M4BL.pdf

Caffentzis, G. and Federici, S. (2014) Commons against and beyond capitalism, *Community Development Journal*, 49(1): 92–105.

Cohen, D. A. (2018) *Climate Justice and the Right to the City, Current Research on Sustainable Urban Development*, University of Pennsylvania.

DeLuca, S. and Rosen, E. (2022) Housing insecurity among the poor today, *Annual Review of Sociology*, 343–71.

Echeverria, F., Gordon, L., Majid, M., Rupani, S. and Samara, T.R. (2018) *Rooted in Home: Community Based Alternatives to the Bay Area Housing Crisis*, Urban Habitat and East Bay Community Law Center.

Fullilove Thompson, M. (2016) *Root Shock: How Tearing Up City Neighborhoods Hurts Americans and What We Can Do About It*, New Village Press.

Kirk, C. (2023) *Decarbonzing California: A Guide To Tenant Protections In Building Upgrades/Retrofits Throughout The State*, Strategic Actions for a Just Economy. Available from: https://www.saje.net/wp-content/uploads/2023/09/Decarbonizing-California-Equitably-Report-1.pdf

Red Nation (2021) *Red Deal: Indigenous Actions to Save Our Earth*, Common Notions.

Schlosberg, D. and Collins, L.B. (2014) From environmental to climate justice: climate change and the discourse of environmental justice, *WIREs Climate Change*. Available from: https://doi.org/10.1002/wcc.275

Smith, N. (1996) *The New Urban Frontier: Gentrification and the Revanchist City*, Routledge.

PART VI

Looking forward

SEVENTEEN

Social problems in the age of culture wars

David C. Lane

This volume is intentionally published to coincide with the 2024 presidential election. For past and current members of the Justice 21 Committee, the vision was to provide policy makers and the public with evidence-based solutions to contemporary problems. It is an effort to engage in public sociology that departs from the discipline's traditional structure of creating and diffusing information.

At the same time, while each chapter in the volume addresses a range of issues using scientific knowledge and tools, they are all cultural products. They are the outcome of not just human effort but a multitude of people collectively engaged in the activity of explaining troubling conditions with scientific evidence.[1] These chapters aim to persuade audiences that social scientific solutions can effectively mitigate or manage these problematic conditions. They slightly differ from how social scientists traditionally attempt to distribute their ideas to audiences.

The volume resides among the thousands of other efforts to persuade people that they ought to engage in action to do something about a troubling condition.[2] While the contributors are primarily social scientists and activists, their explanations of troubling conditions must resonate with audiences. Not all audiences will likely be receptive to the definitions, research evidence, and solutions presented to these problems. They may prefer others who use different forms of persuasion and systems of distribution. The production, distribution, consumption, discussion, memory, and preservation of claims are affected by various institutions and organizations that constrain and facilitate this general process.[3] The construction of social problems involves social processes where human actors assign meaning to troubling conditions, what many have called the social constructionist stance toward social issues.[4] It emphasizes the creation and distribution of meanings that assign trouble to conditions.

Understanding social problems during the culture wars involves accounting for the multitude of ways that people produce, distribute, and consume claims.[5] Producers cannot just create any claim. Audiences need to legitimate those claims. These audiences include people who occupy positions in organizations or institutions that either diffuse those claims or respond to troubling conditions. There are usually many others who labor behind the scenes (writers, editors, bosses, underwriters, and so on) who make consequential decisions that affect the social construction of culture war issues. Audiences receive carefully curated messages about the most pressing problems in the United States.

Yet, audiences are active when consuming ideas about troubling conditions. What some audiences may see as an essential issue, others may see as fanciful, harmful, or not even a problem to worry about. Consider some of the pressing culture war issues of the past few years: book bans, bathroom bans, border control, immigration, gun control or gun rights, school choice, and abortion (this list could be much longer). None of these are new problems, yet some audiences respond with enthusiasm and righteousness. Few people argue these are not real problems. Sustaining culture wars relies on how members of segmented (and divergent) audiences consume information about these troubling conditions. People's interpretations of these issues occur in relation to their values, beliefs, and vision for a better society—including the narratives they understand about these issues.

To think of social problems in the age of culture wars means taking a critical stance toward the social processes that sustain culture wars. As James Davison Hunter argues, culture wars are not simply about ideological and political differences but also the ways that media processes amplify those differences in the narratives developed about particular issues.[6] Producers and distributors of culture war claims rely on rhetorical strategies that exaggerate and overemphasize these differences between audiences. They understand they are competing with other claim makers for audience attention. They also have careers to sustain, with a particular reward system for being successful.[7] Unsurprisingly, using emotional narratives to amplify differences between groups effectively sustains culture war issues in production and distribution. Producers construct sets of claims that are likely to resonate with or appease population segments, and they use forms of dissemination that connect with specific audiences. Those producers do not necessarily have to worry about audiences who may critique their ideas, logic, or reasoning because that audience is likely not consuming that form of media. For example, Truth media allows users to construct, disseminate, and consume claims. However, the platform users are generally a narrow segment of the population. Claims about abortion control or the southern border and immigration may find resonance on the Truth platform that would not find the same degree of resonance among other audiences.

Moreover, the institutions and organizations—and the people who occupy positions within them—that provide solutions to these problems have limited resources (time, money, and budgetary constraints, people with specific skills and training, infrastructure, and so on) to respond to all the proposed definitions and solutions to problems. The chapter by Sullivan in the volume illustrates this constraint. An older, institutionalized definition of the Federal Poverty Level is easier to use rather than debate problems with the measure and how to reconstruct it to match inflation over time. The marketplace for attention persists, and organizations and institutions pick particular definitions and solutions to problems. The public can pressure policy makers and government agencies to adopt specific definitions or solutions to problems. In discussing issues and pressuring policy makers, those members of the public may add their meanings to culture war issues that further exacerbate the differences between groups and, too often, reassert group boundaries through otherization. Reception is not a passive process, as consumers quickly transform claims.

This chapter proposes that changes to the systems of cultural production created the organizational and institutional conditions for culture wars, becoming a prominent aspect of social problem-solving and claims-making. Culture wars refer to the symbolic politics between groups in which one or more groups try to impose their values and beliefs upon others. In culture wars, the symbolic interests of controlling another supersede one's material interests. Culture wars are not new phenomena in the United States, but they have become a prominent feature in claimsmaking campaigns.[8] With relative certainty, every November for the past couple of decades, there are a series of stories in popular and mass media about the war on Christmas and how that is reflective of the value conflicts between groups in the United States—a less than subtle reminder that some will not tolerate religious diversity and immigration. At the core of culture wars are conflicts over changes toward equity, justice, and diversity—those who feel threatened and want to retain traditional or religious interpretations of the world.

One way to understand culture wars is as a rhetorical tactic of claimsmakers. The phrase implies a threat to people's existence or something valued. It means that some type of action is justified to stop this threat. At the same time, this rhetoric has far more detrimental effects. In a war, people are on different sides, fighting against "them"—often a dehumanized enemy. The outcomes of wars generally have one side winning and the other losing. Given the diversity of groups in society, this can lead members of one's group to feel as if they are constantly losing a battle in the larger war to another group. It is also a misleading analogy that can lead to violence within the United States. Wars involve state-sanctioned violence, typically fought within protocols and a rigid command structure. Culture wars occasionally incorporate violence or destruction, but it is not in the hands of the state. The behavior of some factions of the pro-life movement is enough to illustrate the harmful effects of audiences viewing themselves as soldiers fighting for a righteous cause.[9]

The war analogy is also not a new rhetorical strategy to motivate people to care about social problems (wars on poverty, crime, or drugs). Wars on problems recognize the state's role in administering resources to alleviate some troubling conditions. However, a culture war implies different meanings than a war on culture. A culture war pits the listener as a victim of some force, and the only way to preserve their way of life is by fighting for their identity and using state-based solutions that promote their group's values and beliefs. A war on a problem happens against a generalized other. A culture war occurs against the audience receiving the claim. The language of culture war is a rhetorical tactic to motivate potential audiences to care about some issue.

Technology

Facilitating part of the rise of culture wars competing with other social problems are changes in technology. In the production of culture literature, technology refers to the tools people use to communicate and the ways those tools provide new options for the creation of culture.[10] The availability and access to computers and smartphones facilitate the production and distribution of claims involving culture war issues. Almost anyone can make any claim they want about some condition. On top of this, there are no hierarchies of editors and so on that filter messages with their decision-making. Such a dynamic appears in websites like 9gag, Gab, and 4chan, and social media like Truth, which tended to be platforms for disseminating alt-right ideas and recruiting followers. Importantly, these sites also functioned as spaces where anyone could react to claims and create content, such as memes, about culture war issues. Facilitating communication with new technology has provided producers better access to potential audiences.

Distribution mechanisms that facilitate claims about culture war issues have changed straightforwardly. While print media and television news still exist, there is 24-hour, on-demand access to any of that content. News agencies recognize the need to compete across many areas to retain followers. Tapping into culture war issues can be predictable in terms of how an audience will respond. Due to this distribution and access, it can easily seem like culture war issues are the most dominant or critical social problems of the day. Many of the issues typically described as culture wars seem more prevalent because we have much more access to them.[11] What seems like an increase in these issues, is that news agencies compete for followers by tapping into issues with emotional resonance.

At the same time, these new technologies have separated audiences into different publics who view culture wars as an "us" versus "them" situation. Many of these claims about culture wars emphasize "us" winning the war while othering "them" who currently have the upper hand. Embedded in some technologies, such as Truth, Twitter (X), or TikTok, are algorithms that operate as rules guiding content delivery to audiences. Humans made technologies that efficiently sort through interests and content. This system of distribution creates "silos of knowledge" or "echo chambers" where a narrow and ideologically similar set of ideas is received and discussed by audiences. The consequence of this process is that it further divides audiences and reduces the likelihood of people engaging in well-intentioned discussions or debates about public issues.

Law and regulation

Laws, regulations, and policies are additional constraints placed on creating and diffusing claims. On the one hand, laws and regulations are the rules that producers, distributors, and consumers play by when engaging in action. When creating culture, laws and regulations shape the available avenues for human action.[12] Ultimately, organizations and institutions orient their goals in relation to these constraints, which is especially important in solutions to culture war problems. One of the most significant legal changes altering the culture wars was the removal of the Fairness Doctrine in 1987. This change enabled media producers to modify the kinds of content that would appear in news media. No longer were 24-hour networks, such as CNN or, many years later, Fox News, obligated by federal restrictions to provide coverage of different political perspectives and their rebuttals toward public issues. Instead, those stations could tailor stories to specific audiences that stoked fears over culture war issues. One change in federal regulation alters the content people can create and distribute to audiences.

On the other hand, laws and regulations are a goal of some culture war audiences and activists. Culture war issues are often about establishing symbolic control over a group of outsiders. Changing or altering laws can make life more difficult to navigate, especially if those laws diminish people's autonomy. One of the most significant issues of the culture wars has centered on women's access to health care and the right to abortion. Recent legislative decisions at the federal and state levels emphasize moral definitions over medical and scientific explanations and solutions to the problem. This is occurring with bathroom bills, generally about restroom segregation by biological sex. Moral arguments invoke fears that anyone can switch genders on a whim with the intent of harming others in public restrooms. However, the debates over bathroom usage and gender are not entirely new. In the late 1880s, no state-level or federal policies required public restrooms for women, including working women. Today, few argue that public toilets for women contribute toward moral decay or sexual assault. Yet, these familiar narratives reappear as part of the contemporary culture wars around sex and gender in the form of advocates supporting various types of bathroom bills. Establishing laws is an effort to resolve troubling conditions, but most importantly, it is about institutionalizing symbolic control over another.

Finally, various organizational policies affect the content of claims about social problems. Take, for example, the platform TikTok, which has developed quite strict community guidelines for how participants can discuss mental health, suicide, and self-harm. The effects of this policy are that users build their own sets of language to discuss the same troubling conditions. As of this writing, the generally used term for suicide and other forms of death is unalive. These new language uses matriculate into other social problems, as users discuss police officers *unaliving* BIPOC. Users create new meanings and language to avoid banning, moderating, or censoring their content. Policies at the organizational level change the available meanings that claimsmakers and audiences assign to troubling conditions when they engage in social behavior on these platforms.

Industry structure

The literature on cultural production also explains how the structure of industries restricts or facilitates the types of products people create and their pathways for diffusion.[13] This aspect concerns the field and how changing technologies alter the production process and develop new avenues for additional actions. Similarly, social problems claims are cultural creations. The structure of the social problems industry is varied, and this variation contributes to the wide range of claims about the culture wars. Several technological changes (the internet, affordable digital recording and editing, and social media platforms) allowed more people to be more active in claimsmaking. While these processes have allowed almost anyone to have a voice, they have allowed those with extreme or outsider views to reach new audiences. There is simply more content to consume than in previous decades, resulting from changes in the overall field of claimsmaking.

There are consequences of the field accommodating more claimsmakers. For some, this means increased competition for audiences. Presenting issues as personal grievances, a widely used rhetorical tactic of culture war claims, effectively secures vast audience attention. In the spring of 2023, claimsmakers argued that Bud Light, America's #1 selling beer, was betraying the values of its consumers. The rationale was that Dylan Mulvaney promoted the beer. The brand undermined consumer values by allowing someone who is transgender to promote their product. Within a few days, people began posting reaction videos of themselves on Twitter and TikTok, calling for a boycott of the product. Of course, claimsmakers tied these actions to the larger culture war against the threats of change, diversity, "wokeism", and cultural Marxism. This changing field of production also includes many smaller firms competing with prominent producers and distributors of claims. Some smaller firms find a considerable following in niche markets, often focusing on creating claims ordinarily not endorsed by the dominant news media. Firms like The Palmer Report, The Blaze, and One America News Network tap into these niche markets and sustain followings by developing news stories about culture war issues. Glenn Beck initially created and funded The Blaze to appease a small segment of consumer demands. The field itself produces the conditions for claimsmakers to tap into the anxieties of potential audiences. It also creates conditions for audiences to come across many more types of claims.

Organizational structure

An additional element of this model involved the levels of social organization in the production, distribution, and consumption stages of claims. The more complex the social organization, the more capacity to carry out some type of action. An isolated individual can make claims about the war on Christmas, but due to accumulated resources, a large, complex organization has more capacity to disseminate a claim to audiences. There are probably thousands, if not millions, of claims that can exist about culture war issues. Not all claimsmakers have the same resources to develop an effective campaign to alert others.

A similar pattern occurs when policies emerge to manage troubling conditions. Governments tend to have well-funded organizations better equipped to manage troubling conditions than small organizations or individuals. Expending resources is for attention and to get policies implemented. For some advocates, controlling apparatuses of the state is an effective way to engage in a culture war. In just 2 years, the state of Florida passed bills addressing critical race theory in public education, requiring people to use the bathrooms of their biological sex, and a bill reducing the legal statutes for abortion care from 24 weeks to 15 weeks. The organizational structure of the state legislature facilitated the passage of these bills as solutions to culture war issues. Advocates introduced similar versions of these bills in state houses across the country. At the core of these bills is a concern for defining and controlling an "other" whose values threaten one's own group.

Occupational careers

Within any arena of claimsmaking, people have careers. The fields in which a cultural producer or distributor labors will have generally accepted norms that influence how a person's career progresses.[14] Organizational pressures of employment may affect the types of claims one can make about issues. There are a multitude of ways these careers can evolve. They can be long, short, or some duration between those two poles. A short career may consist of a single, failed claimsmaking effort. Not everyone can develop a lengthy career in creating or distributing claims since they need resources to succeed (time, money, interest, and so on). Keeping the attention of audiences is a challenging accomplishment.

Some people sustain careers based on their ability to create claims or endorse issues that resonate with audiences. There are various social moments and countermovement activists who become the charismatic face of cultural war issues. Greta Thunberg (environmental movement), Richard Spencer (alt-right), and Andrew Tate (alpha male movement) all became prominent claimsmakers within their respective movements. This process gives these claimsmakers a degree of status among specific audiences and enables them to distribute claims effectively. Historically, some claimsmakers have been able to carve out careers as leaders or entrepreneurs of social movements. Visibility also restricts some of the ways that construct claims, as the most visible are more likely to receive criticism from their opposition. Recently, factions of the anti-environmental movement have engaged in culture wars through their claimsmaking. While their careers occur in conjunction with think tanks, investigative reporters have found the funding for these careers has ties to the fossil fuels industry.[15] Various capitalists and industries have long funded the sources of financing for careers at think tanks. Similarly, advertisers targeting potential consumers have facilitated careers by financing news production. There are many pathways that careers can take, but success in the competition for followers is essential for sustaining them.

Within more bureaucratic structures, considerable time and status issues affect careers. Commentators in news media have career trajectories, and throughout, they will disseminate many different types of claims. Some, such as Tucker Carlson or Tomi Lahren, have spent considerable proportions of their careers focusing on culture war issues. Often unnoticed is that these commentators have many staff working behind the scenes, which is necessary to produce television news. Scriptwriters, editors, camera operators, postproduction personnel, and bosses construct claims. These people have careers within a hierarchical structure and commit professions and occupations. Specific individuals often receive blame for stoking culture wars. Still, those individuals rely on resources and staff working behind the scenes to package claims in an entertaining format for audiences.

Even politicians recognize the importance of quick-witted soundbites that own the other side for sustaining followers. Tactics that may seem outlandish, unprofessional, and even ethically dubious gain traction with some audience segments. Again, this strategy is not entirely new; as Weber noted in *Politics as Vocation*, a considerable amount of labor for politicians centers on being a charismatic and appealing candidate to voters in future elections.[16] One successful strategy involves maintaining a sizable audience of prospective voters by making statements emphasizing culture war issues. A quick laugh or confirmation of which side the politician is fighting for may be all that is needed to gain enough votes to sustain a career in politics. Careers in culture wars exist because people can retain audiences of followers.

The market

One narrative about the culture wars involves blaming particular claimsmakers or news organizations for duping audiences into believing these are essential issues. That explanation is too simplistic as it assumes that audiences for claims about culture war issues accept them at face value. It presumes that individuals in the audience cannot generate their thoughts and ideas about troubling conditions. This view neglects that creators of culture attempt to satisfy consumer demands in this process. Many cultural creators attempt to account for consumer tastes and interests when developing products.[17] Sustaining careers, movements, and organizations involves targeting existing markets for products or locating new niches.

Targeting existing markets involves developing rhetorical strategies with a degree of predictability. For claimsmakers, this means scanning for existing forms of cultural tension and then developing claims that will remind audiences about their feelings on a particular issue. Thus, many of the culture war issues are not new, and over the past few years, claims have blamed cities and city life for causing the conditions that contribute to social problems. They tend to infer that a more agricultural, rural, or traditional lifestyle would reduce these problems, a kind of antimodernism that both Earnest Hooten and William Sheldon endorsed, with the latter also endorsing strong antisemitic views.[18] Such an overgeneralization about a group of others affecting traditions is not just a classic example. There is a market of consumers who want to hear that LGBT+ identities threaten social order and undermine collective values. These types of culture war claims resonate because producers recognize a consumer market. Most culture war issues are reflective of longstanding values and beliefs toward immigration, diversity, race, gender and sexuality, and fear of change.

Conclusion

This chapter argues that claims about troubling conditions are cultural products. Claims result from many people collaborating to establish definitions of a problematic condition and propose solutions. Those who define them as trouble work within social organizations and institutions that facilitate or constrain the production and distribution of this knowledge to audiences.

Claims involving culture war issues are rooted in symbolic politics and intended for specific audiences. What matters is not being a victim or losing the culture war, and encouraging people to endorse ideas or solutions that may not be in their material interests. It may even include rejecting scientific explanations. Most detrimental is how the distribution and consumption of these ideas reduce democratic discussions of public issues. As this chapter illustrates, the field itself reaches audiences through media technology, segmented into silos of knowledge discussing problems. To some extent, this encourages people to support ideas not in their material interests or follow scientific evidence to depict troubling conditions and their solutions.

Understanding social problems during the culture wars involves accounting for the multitude of ways that claims can be produced, distributed, and consumed by audiences.[19] At each stage, some elements constrain and facilitate particular claims and their likelihood of success. This volume illustrates the process. Scholars and activists produced these chapters. They had specific limitations (such as chapter structure, word counts, types of evidence used, rhetorical form, and so on) and factors like editors who both facilitate and constrain the production of each chapter. Authors make tough decisions and choose a maximum of ten key readings at the end of their chapters—a challenging constraint given some of these problems have thousands of documents that measure and explain them. A book format, on a university press, may only be accessible to specific audiences, and even those audiences may have training or experiences that make them less likely to adopt the ideas proposed in the chapters. Simultaneously facilitating and constraining the volume is the press and the professional association, which both have access and networks that are a resource deployed to diffuse these ideas to some audiences. All this work is necessary because the aggregate of those working to produce the volume generally understand who their audience will be and what types of persuasion are likely to resonate with that audience.

Sociologists, as a discipline, have a stake in these efforts. While our rhetoric tends to rely on the accumulation of scientific knowledge, we need to be more consistent in developing arguments that deviate from narrow interpretations of that cultural form. The systems we use to produce knowledge about culture war issues are inadequate to reach other audiences—there is not much of an audience for our products outside the profession. Changing this involves developing arguments that will resonate with more audiences. The chapters in this book are an effort at trying to create a product that will have an audience outside of the discipline. The extent to which readers beyond academics engage this volume is one small step in that direction.

Notes

[1] Becker, H. S. ([1982] 2008). *Art Worlds.* Berkeley: University of California Press.

[2] See Hilgartner, S., and Bosk, C. L. (1988). The rise and fall of social problems: a public arenas model. *American Journal of Sociology*, 94(1): 53–78, for a depiction of the social problems marketplace and the competition for attention between claimsmakers.

[3] Peterson, R. A., and Anand, N. (2004) The production of culture perspective. *Annual Review of Sociology*, 30: 311–34. These authors use the following specific language to define this perspective, "The production of culture perspective focuses on how the symbolic elements of culture are shaped by the systems within which they are created, distributed, evaluated, taught, and preserved".

[4] See Spector, M. and Kitsuse, J. I. (1977). *Constructing Social Problems*. Cummings Press.

[5] See note 3—Peterson and Anand (2004) update the model to include six constraints: technology; law and regulation; industry structure; organizational structure; occupational careers; and the market.

[6] Hunter, J. D. (1992) *Culture Wars: The Struggle to Control the Family, Art, Education, Law, and politics in America*. Basic Books, 33–34.

[7] See Crane, D. (1976) reward systems in art, science, and religion. *American Behavioral Scientist*, 19(6): 719–34, for an introduction to the role of reward systems in cultural production.

[8] Hunter (1992) discusses the long history of culture wars largely summarized moralists and religious conservatives opposing changes brought about by liberalization and democratization. See also, Gusfield, J. R. (1986) *Symbolic Crusade: Status Politics and the American Temperance Movement*, 2nd edn, University of Illinois Press, for an extensive case study of social movements opposing immigration and alcohol use as a form of symbolic control.

[9] The Civil Rights Division of the United States Department of Justice routinely updates a report documenting this violence. U.S. Department of Justice, Civil Rights Division (2023). Recent Cases on Violence Against Reproductive Health Care Providers. Available from: https://www.justice.gov/crt/recent-cases-violence-against-reproductive-health-care-providers.

[10] See note 3—Peterson and Anand (2004), pp 314: "Technology provides the tools with which people and institutions augment their abilities to communicate, and changes in communication technology profoundly destabilize and create new opportunities in art and culture".

[11] See Best, J. (2001) Social progress and social problems: toward a sociology of gloom. *The Sociological Quarterly*, 42(1): 1–12, for a more elaborate depiction of the paradox of proliferation.

[12] Peterson and Anand (2004, p 315): "Law and regulation create the ground rules that shape how creative fields develop."

[13] Peterson and Anand (2004, p 316).

[14] See note 1—Becker ([1982] 2008).

[15] Kugman, P. (2023) Climate is now a culture war issue. *The New York Times* [online], August 7. Available from: https://www.nytimes.com/2023/08/07/opinion/climate-is-now-a-culture-war-issue.html

[16] Weber M. (1965). *Politics as a Vocation*. Fortress Press.

[17] See note 3—Peterson and Anand (2004), p 317.

[18] Rafter, N., Posick, C., and Rocque, M. (2016). *The Criminal Brain: Understanding Biological Theories of Crime*, 2nd edn. New York University Press, pp 180–2, 186.

[19] See note 3—Peterson and Anand (2004) update the model to include six constraints: technology; law and regulation; industry structure; organizational structure; occupational careers; and the market.

Afterword

Elroi J. Windsor

In her brilliant collection of essays, *Thick*, Dr. Tressie McMillan Cottom invites readers to engage with scholarly research—and to take this engagement personally,

> The things we touch and smell and see and experience through our senses are how stories become powerful. But I have never wanted to only tell powerfully evocative stories. I have wanted to tell evocative stories that become a problem for power. For that, I draw upon data and research.[1]

Cottom applies sociological research to challenge systemic injustices that deeply affect people in real and intimate ways. Like Cottom, the authors in this collection are interested in addressing social problems. They offer readers stories about the problems, asking you to consider ways we might solve them.

The first version of the *Agenda for Social Justice* was published in 2004. Now, 20 years later, much has changed. Although these changes are not always progressive, they show that another world is possible. For example, we have seen the ways social media can act as a transformative feminist agent, such as what the #MeToo movement exposed. We witnessed the rise of a Movement for Black Lives, where people organizing under Black Lives Matter protested in the streets for an end to racist policing and brutality. And, as I write this Afterword, people around the world are calling for a ceasefire and a free Palestine, pleading for an end to the genocide of Palestinian people who have suffered for decades under Israeli occupation. The problems evidenced in our world are serious, severe, and far-reaching. But in each of these cases, people have mobilized for change. The *Agenda for Social Justice* aims to help us understand how we can effect more change.

The contents of the *Agenda for Social Justice* advance a public sociology. The editors of this *Agenda* curated a collection of chapters where scholars use accessible, jargon-free language to argue for practical actions to be taken throughout different public spheres. The authors in this collection present a case, provide supporting evidence, and recommend strategies to tackle issues that are pervasive in the United States. This is the work that sociologists and other social scientists do, though we have not always been great at communicating our ideas beyond academic circles, or within the communities we work within that already actively engage these topics.

In reading the *Agenda*, I hope you found these recommendations easy to understand and apply to what you are seeing in your everyday life.

In this 2024 *Agenda*, authors hone in on structural barriers to change. The essays explore familiar topics like poverty, immigration, and racism, situating them within the institutions that shape the US—law, media, healthcare, education, and more. Authors invite readers to consider ways to dislodge some of the institutional barriers that entrench injustices. In many ways, the issues explored in this collection are not new. They are not groundbreaking announcements of new phenomena. Instead, they cover longstanding problems in the US and abroad. As deeply embedded matters, these problems have benefited from a lot of attention over the years. However, as society changes, they take on new shapes.

In the last 20 years, we have seen shifts in the ways we talk about these matters. Instead of the criminal "justice" system, for example, advocates for change now more commonly use criminal "legal" system to reflect the more accurate unjust realities of incarceration. And now, supporters of trans healthcare rights and access are more likely to use terms like "gender-affirming care" instead of older, outdated language that can be dehumanizing. Our language evolves to capture the nuances of human experiences with sensitivity and care.

Still, the pushback to these efforts remains strong. In 2022, the U.S. Supreme Court overturned *Roe v. Wade*, setting back reproductive freedoms and dramatically impacting access to abortion services. Currently, politicians in some conservative-leaning states are targeting initiatives designed to promote diversity, equity, and inclusion (DEI), banning DEI efforts in public education. They are also criminalizing medical care for trans youth, even when that care is supported by family members and healthcare providers. These actions remind us that as social justice progresses, opponents will stubbornly try to bat them back. Clearly, more work needs to be done.

It is important to remember that the chapters in this collection are organized under an explicit charge. They fall under the title *Agenda for Social Justice*, where an "agenda" implies *something is to be done*. Each essay in this collection identifies specific measures to be taken that reduce social problems. Authors base their arguments on research, not ideology, citing recent studies that explain why actions must be taken. They outline the harms of inaction and the benefits of change. They contend that these actions are to be taken in pursuit of social justice—the guiding principle of the Society for the Study of Social Problems (SSSP), the organization sponsoring this project in conjunction with Policy Press. As Dr Shirley A. Jackson asked in her Presidential Address at the 2023 SSSP Annual Meetings, "Sociologists study the negative and positive ramifications of social change, but are we doing enough to share this information with non-sociologists, particularly those who might benefit today as well as in the future?"[2] Ultimately, then, the

Agenda for Social Justice is not simply a collection of writings to be passively read, studied, and put down for further reflection. It is a call to act. And you, as a reader, are being asked to engage with a project for social change.

So, reader, what are you going to do?

As you read these chapters, you may have gravitated toward some topics more than others. Consider the topics that resonated with you. Perhaps you related more to certain issues due to your personal experiences or your professional interests. So, what can you do with this information? Perhaps your life's work revolves around specific areas, and those topics drive your focus. It is impossible for each of us to act on all of these problems all of the time. But it is imperative for each of us to take some kind of action when we can.

The solutions to the social problems examined in this volume illustrate that social change is not only possible, but practical. The chapters outline concrete strategies for remedying social problems, from standard recommendations about policy change, legal reform, and education, to more creative solutions, like creating a low/no-cost "food bus" of markets to improve lower-income families' access to quality food.[3] As a reader of this work, you are someone who can take individual action. You may be a voter, a policy maker, a policy analyst, a media creator and consumer. You are likely a member of multiple communities where you can have a say in determining how things go. You may even be in a position of power where you can implement some of these changes directly. After all, it is individuals who make up the institutions that can often feel too impossible and ingrained to shift. So, take those topics that you care about and act. Apply your passion and do something with this knowledge. Put into action the changes these scholars recommend.

Readers, we are not in a meeting, so this *Agenda for Social Justice* is not adjourned. Instead, I hope you let this agenda inform your actions toward creating a more just world.

Notes

[1]   Cottom, T. M. (2019). *Thick: And Other Essays*. The New Press.

[2]   Jackson, S. A. (2024). The 2023 SSSP Presidential Address: Recycled: the emergence and re-emergence of social problems. *Social Problems,* spae002, https://doi.org/10.1093/socpro/spae002.

[3]   See Chapter Nine, this volume.